WILHELM REICH

MODERN MASTERS

Already published

ALBERT CAMUS / Conor Cruise O'Brien
FRANTZ FANON / David Caute
HERBERT MARCUSE / Alasdair MacIntyre
CHE GUEVARA / Andrew Sinclair
CLAUDE LÉVI-STRAUSS / Edmund Leach
LUDWIG WITTGENSTEIN / David Pears
GEORGE LUKÁCS / George Lichtheim
NOAM CHOMSKY / John Lyons
JAMES JOYCE / John Gross
MARSHALL McLUHAN / Jonathan Miller
GEORGE ORWELL / Raymond Williams
SIGMUND FREUD / Richard Wollheim
WILLIAM BUTLER YEATS / Denis Donoghue
MOHANDAS GANDHI / George Woodcock

MODERN MASTERS

EDITED BY frank kermode

wilhelm reich

charles rycroft

NEW YORK | THE VIKING PRESS

CONTENTS

i / Biographical Introduction 1

ii / Energy, Character, and Orgasm 13

iii / Reich and the Sexual Paradise 33

iv / The Sexual Revolution 53

v / Vegetotherapy 67

vi / Orgonomy and Reich's Discovery of God 79

vii / Summing Up 95

Short Bibliography 105

Index 107

WILHELM REICH

Biographical Introduction

i

Although this is not a biography of Reich, some facts of his life have to be mentioned if we are to understand his ideas and place them correctly in history. Reich was born on March 24, 1897, at Dobrzynica in Galicia, but he spent most of his childhood on a farm at Jujinetz in Bucovina. Both Galicia and Bucovina were outlying provinces of the Austro-Hungarian Empire until its collapse at the end of the First World War, and Reich was therefore an Austrian citizen (until he became a naturalized American in 1938), but one whose home country was abroad from 1919 onward.

His family was of Jewish origin, but the Jewish religion and observances played no part in his upbringing. His father was a farmer, and, according to Ilse Ollendorf Reich, the family was "well-to-do, highly respected, somewhat stuck-up and put a very pronounced stress on German culture." They must, then, given the current distinction between master nations and subject peoples prevailing within the Austro-Hungarian Empire, have been representatives if not exactly of an occupying ruling class isolated among colonials, at least of a cultural elite which looked north and west to Berlin and Vienna for its inspirations. Again according to Ilse Ollendorf Reich, he was not allowed to associate with either the local Ukrainian-speaking peasantry or the few Yiddish-speaking Jewish families that lived nearby. He seems to have had a lonely childhood, never even becoming intimate with his only brother, who was three years younger than himself.

However—and his followers make something of this —from his earliest years he was in intimate touch with nature, familiar with the details of the farmyard and cattle breeding, and he learned young to ride and shoot. In this—and in his totally non-Jewish secular upbringing—his childhood was in striking contrast to that of the majority of the intellectuals who were drawn toward psychoanalysis in the 1920s.

Although Reich, one gathers, always spoke nostalgically of the physical surroundings of his childhood and retained throughout his life a great affection and feeling for the countryside, he rarely mentioned his family or reminisced about his childhood. This is hardly surprising in view of the conjunction of private tragedy and political catastrophe which led, while he was in his teens, to the complete disruption of the world he had been brought up in. In 1911, when he was fourteen, his mother committed suicide, apparently after he had revealed to his father that she was having an affair with his tutor. Then his father developed tuberculosis and died three years later. Although Reich was still a schoolboy, he attempted to run the family farm until it became a battlefield. In 1916 he left home and joined the Austrian army, in which he became an officer and saw active service in Italy.

At the end of the war Reich arrived in Vienna, a twenty-one-year-old war veteran, both of his parents dead, and his childhood home (which he never visited again) cut off from him by the new frontiers drawn by the politicians at Versailles. After a brief flirtation with the law he became a student of medicine and decided almost immediately to take up psychiatry. Within a year of arriving in Vienna he became a member of the Vienna Psychoanalytical Society and a practicing psychoanalyst.

To anyone familiar with the contemporary psychoanalytical scene it seems almost incredible that a medical student still in his early twenties should have been allowed to treat patients, or that Reich should have been able to write and get published four papers on psychoanalysis and sexology within three years of his first contact with psychoanalysis. But the psychoanalytical movement was very different then. It had yet to institutionalize training or to insist on a training analysis of several years' duration for all would-be analysts, and Reich was far from being the only medically unqualified person who had patients referred to him by Freud within a few months of first coming into contact with psychoanalysis.[1]

[1] Although Reich became an analyst before experience of being a patient was a required part of every analyst's train-

It should be mentioned here that Reich contributed significantly to the developments in psychoanalysis that transformed it from what in retrospect appears as an amateurish activity into a professional technique that can be taught formally. From 1924 to 1930 he was the director of the Seminar for Psychoanalytic Therapy, in which practical problems of treatment were thrashed out, and three of his papers on technique are included in a volume called *The Psychoanalytic Reader*, which is to this day recommended reading for students at psychoanalytical institutes.

Vienna in the 1920s was very unlike the affluent societies in which psychoanalytical organizations today flourish and can exert considerable control over their students' activities. The former metropolis of a large polyglot empire had suddenly become the capital of a small and impoverished republic. The glory and the tinsel had departed with the Hapsburgs; the hierarchical, largely Catholic and feudal structure of society had collapsed, leaving a void waiting to be filled. It is therefore not surprising that Reich became involved in politics, and he was indeed far from being the only analyst who sought to reconcile psychoanalysis and Marxism. He seems, however, to have been the only one whose activities so antagonized both schools of thought that he was expelled from both the International Psychoanalytical Association and the Communist Party.

---

ing, he had more than one period of being analyzed by more than one analyst. Ilse Ollendorf Reich says of his first analysis, "[It] was broken off by Reich unfinished, as were the following ones." But of a later analysis in Berlin she reports that it ended abruptly when his analyst emigrated to America.

In view of the fact that the history of the psycho-analytical movement has excited more later curiosity than has that of the German and Austrian Communist parties, and that Reich has left more of a mark on psychoanalysis and psychotherapy than on Marxism, more explanations are current as to why Reich became unacceptable to the analysts—or broke with them—than of why he was expelled from the Communist movement. According to Reich himself, his expulsion from the psychoanalytic movement was due to theoretical differences regarding the social implications of psychoanalysis, compounded by professional jealousies, but according to others the cause was more personal. Reich wished to be analyzed by Freud; Freud refused; Reich took his refusal as a personal rejection, became depressed and tuberculous and even, according to his first wife (his third wife disagrees), the victim of a "deteriorating process" from which he never recovered.

Developing a father-fixation on Freud, with resulting therapeutic longings toward him, must have been a serious occupational hazard among the early analysts if this second explanation is correct. A decade earlier another analyst, Viktor Tausk, who like Reich was a nonpracticing Jew from an outlying province of the Austro-Hungarian Empire, was refused an analysis by Freud. According to Paul Roazen's study of Tausk[2] this rejection by Freud initiated a reaction which ended in Tausk's suicide six months later.

Whatever the inner story of Reich's break with Freud

[2] Paul Roazen, *Brother Animal: The Story of Freud and Tausk* (New York: Knopf, 1969). Incidentally, a paper by Tausk also appears in Fliess's *Psychoanalytic Reader*.

and psychoanalysis may be, the following appears to be the correct chronology:

1927. Reich seeks analysis with Freud, who refuses to treat him. The first version[3] of Reich's *The Function of the Orgasm* is published by the International Psychoanalytic Publishing House. Reich spends some months in a Swiss sanatorium.

1928. Reich joins the Austrian Communist Party. With four other analysts and three obstetricians he founds the Socialist Society for Sex Consultation and Sexological Research.

1929. Reich visits Russia. His *Dialectical Materialism and Psychoanalysis* is published in Moscow.

1930. Reich moves to Berlin. He founds the German Association for Proletarian Sexual Politics, whose aims include the abolition of laws against abortion and homosexuality and the dissemination of birth-control information.

1933. Reich publishes *The Mass Psychology of Fascism* in Denmark. He is expelled from the German Communist Party. The first version of Reich's *Character Analysis* is printed by the International Psychoanalytical Publishing House but without its imprint.

1934. Reich is expelled or, rather, "dropped" or "edged out" of the International Psychoanalytical Association— the details of this process are too complicated and obscure to be worth elucidating.

In retrospect neither of the two expulsions seems in-

[3] "Version," not "edition." Reich had the bibliographically maddening habit of completely rewriting books for their later editions, or to put it the other way round, of giving old titles to entirely new books.

tellectually justified, though in view of the political circumstances of the time they are perhaps forgivable. The psychoanalytical movement felt it had no chance of surviving the rise of fascism if it was associated with Communism—the German Psychoanalytical Society several times asked Reich to resign for this reason but he always refused—while the Communist Party felt Reich was diverting energies into mental and sexual hygiene campaigns which were required for direct political action. But, in the event, the psychoanalytical movement's hope of riding the storm of fascism by claiming to be a pure science and unpolitical proved illusory, and the defeat of the Communist and socialist movements by fascism can hardly be lain at the door of Reich's diversions into sexology. Nor, in retrospect, do the psychoanalytical movement's objections to the first version of Reich's *Character Analysis* seem justifiable or intellectually comprehensible; almost all of it had already appeared previously in psychoanalytical journals and the decision to withhold official blessing seems to have been based solely on grounds of political expediency.

From now on Reich was on his own. He was a member of no established organization, and his ideas had been rejected by two movements to which he had given himself wholly. From now on, too, anyone who attempts to follow the development of his ideas is in serious difficulties. Either he continues to take Reich seriously, in which case he runs the risk of being converted to a way of thinking which would put him, in Reich's own words, "beyond the intellectual framework of present-day character structure and, with that, the civilization of the last 5,000 years," or he ceases to do so, in which case he runs the risk of falling into the methodological trap of using Reich's personality as an argument against his ideas. Even Reich's greatest admirers admit that he was a difficult and autocratic man, and it is not hard to point to aspects of his life and writings that call his sanity into question—the two possible psychiatric diagnoses are hypomania for his early years and paranoia for his later—but there are, it seems to me, several objections to using this all too easy way out.

First, if Reich *was* right and he really did "step beyond the intellectual framework of present-day character structure," diagnostic labels that derive from this intellectual framework are inapplicable to him—or indeed to anyone else. Society's views on who is sane and who is mad obviously depend to a large extent on its criteria of normality, and as a result anyone who questions its norms runs the risk of being considered mad. All prophets, world-shakers, and dreamers of dreams are at risk in this way, and indeed a large number of them have been manhandled by psychiatrists and analysts foolish enough to rush in where angels fear to tread. Jesus Christ has been diagnosed schizophrenic, Beethoven paranoid, the Old Testament prophets (collectively) schizophrenoid, Leonardo da Vinci schizoid-obsessional, etc., etc. Although psychiatric excursions of this kind are not always without interest, they suffer from two grave limitations. They assume that contemporary psychoanalytical theory has achieved timeless objectivity, that the criteria by which we now assess human personality are independent of the historical processes that have led to the emergence of the Freudian conception of human nature; and they fail to escape from the reductionist tendencies built into psycho-analytical theories and therefore in effect if not in intention tend to invalidate the ideas produced by the individuals subjected to this sort of treatment. It seems to me that no amount of study of the origins of new ideas in the minds of those who first formulated them helps one to make the crucial decision, whether these ideas are true or false. Both true and false prophets must have had their infantile traumata, their Oedipus complexes, and their neuroses.

Fortunately Reich made one claim for his ideas that simplifies matters enormously for anyone attempting to assess them. He claimed to have discovered not only the truths about the nature of energy and of love, but also that these truths were demonstrable by the techniques of the natural sciences. His truths were not poetic or religious or artistic truths but scientific truths which could, he claimed, be confirmed by anyone who repeated his experiments. Anyone who attempts to evaluate his ideas is therefore entitled to use as critical weapons the available evidence bearing on such questions as: 1) Did Reich understand the nature of scientific method? 2) Did he have a good and thorough knowledge of biology and physics, the two sciences on which he leaned most heavily? 3) Did he construct his experiments with scientific rigor and with proper respect for the need for controls? 4) Have his ideas on physics and biology attracted sympathetic interest among those experts best qualified to understand and assess them? All these are legitimate questions to ask since in one respect Reich certainly did not "step beyond the intellectual framework of present-day human character structure." Although he became increasingly interested in aspects of human nature that have traditionally been the domain of the humanities and even of religious mysticism, he retained throughout his life the belief that rationalism and the natural sciences are the only avenues to the truth.

Although the answers to the four questions I posed above must be "No," or so it seems to me, this does not, I believe, dispose of Reich. He might after all have been wrong in supposing that all truths are natural-scientific truths, and yet have arrived at insights of value. Even if he was wrong in believing that the methods of natural science are appropriate for the study of human nature, some at least of his ideas might be valid, even if misplaced and ill-based. What I am suggesting here, and hope to substantiate later, is that Reich was barking up the wrong tree and that his allegiance to the natural sciences compelled him to deceive himself into believing that his ideas about energy, love, and the cosmos were the result of his scientific researches when in fact they were the product of some inner process of development that led him to conclusions that a number of poets, mystics, and theologians have reached by subjective and largely introspective routes. In so deceiving himself he developed to an absurdity a tendency also present in Freud, who consistently converted the insights into human nature that he gained through his self-analysis and from his professional association with neurotic patients into objective and impersonal-sounding theories intended to satisfy the criteria of the natural sciences.

After this digression I must return to my summary account of Reich's life, though I must confess to a certain sense of unreality about doing so. This derives from two sources. First, Reich's career and ideas up to the mid-1930s are clearly related to time and place. His interest in psychoanalysis could only have developed and taken the form it did in Vienna in the 1920s, and it constitutes a contribution to an intellectual movement which began before he entered it and which continues into the present. Similarly his Marxism and his political activities are inexplicable without references to the social tragedy by which he and all those close to him were overwhelmed. But after 1934 his ideas take a private course; he has followers who accept his ideas, usually after having been his patients, but no external influences seem to work on him, and as a result it seems irrelevant to know which of his ideas and therapeutic innovations date from his stay in Denmark, which first saw the light of day during the two years he spent in Norway, and which date from after 1938 when he settled in the United States. It is, however, important to know that in the United States his therapeutic practice was sufficiently successful to provide him with funds to conduct his researches on an extensive scale, to found journals, and to set up a foundation for the propagation of his ideas and a Wilhelm Reich Infant Trust Fund for their advancement after his death.

Finally, I must mention his trial and death in prison, since these are events which play an important part in the mythology that surrounds Reich. By the 1950s Reich had persuaded himself that it was possible to isolate life energy in the form of vesicles, which he called bions, and to store it in accumulators known as orgone boxes. He also believed that it was possible to cure patients with cancer and other diseases by placing them inside these boxes. In 1954 the United States Food and Drug Administration placed an injunction against the distribution of orgone boxes on the ground that the claims made on their behalf were fraudulent. Reich refused either to obey the injunction or to recognize the competence of the courts to adjudicate on matters of scientific fact. He was eventually charged with contempt of court and sentenced to two years' imprisonment. After imprisonment he was diagnosed paranoid and transferred to "the only penitentiary with psychiatric treatment facilities," where he was, however, declared "legally sane and competent." On November 3, 1957, he died of heart disease.

Energy, Character, and Orgasm

ii

Reich's ideas about energy, character, and orgasm can only be understood in the light of their origin in the kind of psychoanalysis that he encountered in Vienna in the 1920s. At that time psychoanalysis was still under the unquestioned influence of Freud's ideal of a psychological theory that would satisfy all the criteria of a natural science.

As a young man Freud had worked as a physiologist under Ernst Brücke, who was a leading member of a crusading antivitalist scientific movement usually known as the Helmholtz School of Medicine. The aims of this school are epitomized by a "solemn oath" pledged in 1842 by Brücke and his fellow physiologist Du Bois-Reymond.

No other forces than the common physical and chemical ones are active within the organism. In those cases which cannot at present be explained by these forces one either has to find the specific way or form of their action by means of the physical-mathematical method or to assume new forces equal in dignity to the chemical-physical forces inherent in matter, reducible to the force of attraction and repulsion.

The Helmholtz school was reductionist and both anti-idealist and antireligious. It was concerned to ensure that religious and vitalist concepts such as "spirit," "*élan vital*," "life force" were excluded from the biological sciences and to demonstrate that the structure and behavior of living organisms were explicable solely in terms of the concepts of physics and chemistry. Its standpoint was strictly determinist and assumed that all explanations are in terms of causation; it seems to have been strangely untroubled by the possibility that the emergence of consciousness, and in man of reflective self-awareness, might pose awkward problems when it came to applying causal-deterministic modes of thought to the behavior of man and the higher animals.

Inspired by this ideal, Freud's lifelong ambition was to construct a scientific psychology in which mental phenomena could be shown to be subject to the laws of causation and to be reducible to a number of simple statements about the forces of attraction and repulsion operating within a system or structure consisting of mental units or "ideas." He assumed that there exists some form of mental energy which, as he wrote in 1894, "possesses all the characteristics of quantity (though we have no means of measuring it), which is capable of increase, diminution, displacement, and discharge, and which is spread over the memory traces of ideas somewhat as an electric charge is spread over the surface of a body."[1] He assumed further that this mental energy circulated within a mental apparatus, which was conceived to have structure. In Freud's original formulations this structure consisted of a conscious and an unconscious, but in 1923, with the publication of *The Ego and the Id*, the mental apparatus became tripartite, consisting of an id, an ego, and a superego. Ideas, impulses, emotions, etc., were conceived to be located at specific points in this apparatus; changes in feeling, desire, and thought were explained as the result of movements of quanta of energy from one part of the mental apparatus to another; while actions were conceived to be accompanied by discharge of energy.

Despite the fact that Freud's "scientific psychology" is patently a form of science fiction, with its quanta of unquantifiable energy and its transposition of temporal relationships into spatial ones (in the mental apparatus, the past is underneath the present and ideas move upward as they became conscious), in Freud's own writings it sounds very scientific and objective and Freud's followers in the 1920s seem, with the possible exceptions of Lou Andreas-Salomé and Oscar Pfister, to have been entirely oblivious of the complications produced by the fact that the data that it purported to explain were subjective phenomena derived from introspection and reminiscence. They seem to have accepted without question Freud's assumption that the translation of human

[1] *Standard Edition of the Complete Psychological Works of Sigmund Freud* (New York: Macmillan, 1964–   ), III.

experience into the language of the natural sciences was a worthwhile activity and not, as many analysts now believe, an unprofitable if sometimes amusing game.

Since Reich's later researches were primarily concerned with the nature of biological energy, two of Freud's ideas about mental energy must be mentioned briefly. First, he held that it existed in two forms, one mobile and the other "bound," mobile energy being characteristic of unconscious mental processes, which were regarded as "chaotic" and unstructured, bound energy being characteristic of conscious mental processes, which were regarded as having structure and organization. Since Freud also held that mental energy has its origin in bodily processes, this idea that mind consists of energy existing in two forms bears a remarkable resemblance to Blake's statement that "energy is the only life and is from the body; and reason is the bound and outward circumference of energy."

Second, Freud usually, though not quite always, equated general mental energy and erotic energy, "libido." Here again his thinking is curiously similar to Blake's "energy is eternal delight." However, despite the similarities between Freud's and Blake's views on the nature of mental energy, they differ fundamentally in respect of their origins and credentials. Blake reached his insight by an admitted act of poetic imagination, while Freud claimed to have reached his by scientific observation and reasoning.

Although Freud's first theories about mental energy and structure, which are described in his *Project for a Scientific Psychology*, written in 1895 but only published posthumously, were formulated in the hope that they would prove to correspond precisely with the way the brain works, he later saw clearly that his mental apparatus was a fiction, a metaphorical system that did not necessarily bear any real relation to the physiological and neurological processes accompanying and underlying mental activity. However, like all analogies, it could and often was taken literally by the philosophically unwary, and I think that there can be little doubt that Reich believed in the objective reality of Freud's mental apparatus.

However, despite his acceptance of the mechanist assumptions underlying the idea of the mental apparatus, Reich was also a vitalist, both by temperament and conviction. In the early 1920s he read a lot of Bergson, acquiring indeed the reputation of being a "crazy Bergsonian," and in the biographical chapter of the 1942 version of *The Function of the Orgasm* there is a revealing passage which shows that he always wanted to replace ideas by things and to resolve the vitalist-mechanist antithesis by discovering some "tangible" *thing* in which the life force could be located.[2]

As we shall see, Reich eventually persuaded himself that he had succeeded in reconciling the vitalist intuitive perception of a life force with the mechanist appeal to the intellect by discovering a substance, which could be touched and "practically handled," in which the life force was embodied.

Just as Reich's ideas on life energy derive from Freud's ideas on mental energy and libido, so too his

[2] See *The Function of the Orgasm*, pp. 6–7.

ideas on "character" can be traced back to Freud's concept of "defense."

According to Freud, unconscious ideas and wishes do not just happen to be unconscious. On the contrary, they strive energetically to become conscious but are prevented from becoming so by the action of "defense mechanisms," the best known and first described of these mechanisms being repression. In other words, the mind, the mental apparatus, is assumed to be divided into two parts, an instinctual part which strives for self-expression and for recurrent discharge of its accumulating energies, and another "reasonable" part which is concerned to maintain its equilibrium and to avoid tension, stress, and anxiety. If the wishes of the former part, the id, are felt to threaten the latter part's equilibrium or to endanger its relation to the outside world (by instigating actions that will be met by frustration, opposition, or social and moral disapproval), this latter part, the ego, will attempt to protect itself from the anticipated distress and to ensure itself against disappointment and disapproval by activating defenses that prevent the disturbing impulse from becoming conscious.

There is, it will be noted, something ambiguous about this conception of the mind as a structure inherently divided against itself. The equilibrium-seeking part, the ego, is conceived to suffer from divided loyalties. On one hand, it wishes to experience the joys and pleasures of self-expression, of "instinctual satisfaction"; on the other hand, it seeks to accommodate itself to the limitations of the environment it finds itself in and to the moral values of the society of which it is a member.

Moreover, since the ego is held to internalize (or identify with) these moral values and to construct within itself a third structure, the superego, whose inner commands it feels impelled to obey, the unfortunate ego is conceived to have the unenviable task of trying to reconcile three often incompatible sets of demands—those of the id, those of the superego, and those of the environment.

Now, although this theory purports to be scientific and morally neutral, and although too it can be used to describe and classify neurotic states in terms of such concepts as "the strength of the instincts," "the severity of the superego," "the strength of the ego," etc., the practical conclusions drawn from it are likely to depend to a considerable extent on the personality and temperament of the person using it. If he is an optimist who holds that man is basically good and if he sets a high value on self-expressive activity, he is likely to be pro-id and will tend to regard the superego and social morality as the villains of the piece; while if he is a pessimist convinced of man's evil and destructiveness, he will tend to side with the ego's struggle to master and control its unruly instinctual endowment.

It would be convenient and dramatically satisfying if it were possible to maintain that Freud was basically a pessimist opposed to the instincts and Reich an optimist wholeheartedly on the side of instinctual self-expression. This opposition is indeed sometimes assumed by Reich's followers, but it is, I think, unfair to both Freud and Reich.

Freud did, it is true, sometimes write very negatively about the id, which he once described as a "cauldron of seething excitations," while in *Civilization and Its Dis-*

contents he developed the thesis that the development of all culture and civilization is unavoidably based on instinctual renunciation. However, he seems also to have held that instinctual renunciation involves a real and regrettable loss—i.e., his theory of culture is ironical and tragic and not ascetic—and in his paper "Civilized Sexual Morality and Modern Nervousness" he stated unequivocally his conviction that our own (or rather his, since this paper was written in 1908) civilization demands more renunciation of its members than is necessary for its preservation. As Ernest Jones said of this paper, "It was in essence a protest against the exorbitant demands of society, especially in the sexual sphere, on the life of the individual. The grounds of this protest are as valid now as then, but in some respects the paper has an interest as a period piece. It depicts a civilization in many ways different from our present one, and it can be said that some of the important changes in the past half-century are the direct result of Freud's own work."[3]

[3] Ernest Jones, *The Life and Work of Sigmund Freud* (New York: Basic Books, 1955), II, 328. The idea that civilization is based on instinctual renunciation was a conclusion that seemed to follow inevitably from Freud's theory of sublimation, but I doubt whether many contemporary analysts subscribe to it. According to Freud's theory of sublimation, all "higher" mental functions evolve out of "lower" physical ones, use energy which in the first instance belongs to these lower ones, and only develop insofar as the channels of expression of the lower, physical functions are blocked by frustration and repression. Modern psychoanalysis has extricated itself from the impasse created by this theory by postulating that the ego, in which higher mental functions are conceived to be located, has its own sources of energy independent of the id, and that "sublimations" are inbuilt tendencies that emerge spontaneously under favorable conditions, although experiences of "delay in satisfaction" are

Nor, although Reich certainly was an optimist who believed that inside every corrupted, civilized man there was a Rousseauan Noble Savage trying to escape, is it true that he believed in instinctual freedom in the sense of supposing that each and every desire should be acted upon immediately. Although he held that sexual deprivation produced states of "sexual stasis" that provided the energy with which neuroses are engendered and perpetuated, his conceptions of sexual potency and satisfaction included the necessity of total involvement of the personality in sexual relationships. He also maintained that the truly healthy man, the so-called "genital character," possessed a natural internal regulating function that makes socially enforced "compulsive morality" unnecessary.

> The healthy individual has no compulsive morality because he has no impulses which call for moral inhibition. . . . Intercourse with a prostitute becomes impossible. Sadistic phantasies disappear. To expect love as a right or even to rape a sexual partner becomes inconceivable, as do ideas of seducing children. Anal, exhibitionistic or other perversions disappear, and with these the social anxiety and guilt feelings. The incestuous fixation to parents and siblings loses its interest; this liberates the energy which was bound up in such fixations. In brief, all these phenomena point to the fact that the organism is capable of *self-regulation.*[4]

In this connection it is amusing to note that in one passage in *The Function of the Orgasm* Reich expresses

---

perhaps necessary for their development. See Heinz Hartmann, *Ego Psychology and the Problem of Adaptation* (New York: International Universities Press, 1958).

[4] *The Sexual Revolution*, pp. 6–7.

with such definiteness his conviction that "genital characters" are moral that his American translator found it
necessary to insert a footnote designed to reassure
readers that Reich did not believe in lifelong monogamy;
but only that sexual relationships, while they last, constitute a bond to which neither partner wishes to be
unfaithful.[5]

Freud's idea that the ego defends itself against impulses arising in the id leads naturally to the idea that
a person's "character" may be a defense, and to the
clinical concept that in addition to psychoneurotics
whose symptoms are the result of conflict between repressed and repressing aspects of their personality, there
are also "character neurotics" whose habitual stances
and attitudes are interpretable as defenses against un-
welcome, unconscious instinctual tendencies. In such
people character traits are the equivalents of symptoms,
since they are compulsive, involuntary patterns of behavior whose function it is to prevent the emergence of
repressed impulses. Examples of such character defenses are habitual submissiveness and obsequiousness
preventing the emergence of envy and hostility, habitual
solicitousness covering cruelty, and habitual assertiveness acting as a defense against unconscious wishes to
be passive and dependent.

This idea that a person's "character," in the sense of
his habitual, stereotyped attitudes and responses to
situations, is a defense has become an essential part of
every analyst's intellectual equipment, but Reich cannot
be credited with it, since it can be traced back in the

[5] See *The Function of the Orgasm*, translator's note, p. 152.

psychoanalytical literature at least as far as 1908, when Freud published his *Character and Anal Erotism*. Reich does, however, seem to have been the first analyst to appreciate that it might be possible and indeed necessary to treat patients by interpreting the nature and functions of their character rather than by analyzing their dreams and free associations. Even when he was a conventional analyst he took the view that it was a waste of time listening to a patient's free association or interpreting his dreams unless the analyst had previously made him aware of his habitual attitude of, say, submissiveness or rudeness toward the analyst and had succeeded in getting him to understand why he found it necessary to relate to him in such a stereotyped way. Only after this had been made clear to the patient could he, in Reich's view, become at ease and spontaneous with his analyst and open up sincerely to him in a way that made his free associations valid communications.

Reich's advocacy of character analysis in addition or in preference to symptom analysis and dream interpretation also contributed to the realization that the therapeutic effect of psychotherapy derives not from the unearthing of traumatic memories or from the correct interpretation of dreams and symptoms but from the nature of the relationship which develops between analyst and patient. By insisting on the importance of analyzing the patient's defenses against spontaneous rapport between himself and the analyst, Reich opened up the possibility of discovering what really goes on between them and contributed significantly to the idea that psychotherapy consists in a confrontation or encounter between two real, live people. As a result his work constitutes a formative though not always acknowledged influence, not only on contemporary psychoanalysis with its emphasis on the importance of transference and countertransference interactions, but also on the existentialist, contractual, and "encounter" schools of psychotherapy.[6]

However, Reich was not content to stop here. He soon went further, maintaining that character was *the* essential defense in *all* cases and that civilized Western man was imprisoned in a character armor that prevented him from expressing his spontaneous feelings of love and hatred in general, and from experiencing orgasm in particular. This character armor represented the precipitation within his personality of society's antiemotional, antilibidinal "compulsive morality," the origins of which Reich explained in terms of his social and political theories. These are discussed later in Chapter III.

Reich's theory of orgasm also has its roots in Freud's thinking. According to Freud (1894) the neuroses could be divided into two groups, actual neuroses and psychoneuroses; the former being the direct, physiological result of present-day (*aktuel*) disturbances of sexual function, the latter being complicated, psychological consequences of past experiences. Actual neuroses, being of physiological origin, were incapable of psychological interpretation and did not require it; they were cured automatically if the patient abandoned unhealthy sexual habits such as excessive masturbation, coitus interruptus, or abstinence. On the other hand the psycho-

[6] See particularly the writings of R. D. Laing, Rollo May, Alexander Lowen, and F. S. Perls.

neuroses, being complex psychological formations, could only be explained and cured by psychoanalytical investigation and interpretation of the patient's Oedipus complex and infantile sexual phantasies and by the recovery of repressed traumatic experiences.

Although this distinction between actual and psychoneuroses was in theory simple and straightforward, in practice matters were more complicated. If one sought to explain why any particular patient allowed himself to develop an actual neurosis, it often became necessary to postulate the simultaneous presence of a psychoneurosis that prevented him from organizing for himself a satisfactory sex life; while, since psychoneuroses lead to sexual inhibitions, they were bound to be compounded by a superimposed actual neurosis.

As a result some analysts denied the usefulness of the distinction, while even more denied the existence of the actual neuroses and sought to explain all neuroses and all neurotic anxiety in purely psychological terms. Reich, however, took the opposite stance, maintaining that an actual neurosis formed the core of every psychoneurosis, and that actual neuroses had a psychoneurotic superstructure. Furthermore, he argued, it was the inability of psychoneurotics to discharge sexual energy completely and with satisfaction during orgasm that created the damming up of energy (the "sexual stasis" in his terminology) that kept the psychoneurosis alive. In other words, he thought that neurotics were caught in a vicious circle. Their actual neurosis provided the energy to create and maintain their psychoneurosis, which then perpetuated their actual neurosis.

This view of the relationship between actual and psychoneuroses has not been absorbed into psychoanalytical thinking, but it has two great merits. It retains a connection between psychopathology and physiology—in the last resort the neuroses are not purely mental formations but arise from and affect the body—and it provides an explanation of why neuroses do not disappear spontaneously. So far as I know Reich is the only analyst to offer any sort of explanation as to why the childhood pathogenic experiences that according to psychoanalysis cause neuroses do not gradually lose their impact when neurotics move away from their childhood environment.

Now, since, as Reich himself readily admitted, many psychoneurotics appeared or claimed to be living normal and satisfactory sex lives, his position compelled him to call into question the normality and authenticity of much that passes for normal sex. In particular, he challenged the idea that orgastic potency could be defined simply in terms of the capacity for erection, penetration, and ejaculation (and *mutatis mutandis* for women). These capacities were, he maintained, only "the indispensable prerequisites" for orgastic potency. True orgastic potency involved much more and excluded much that passed for normal. It involved, *inter alia*, the capacities for uninhibited surrender to the flow of biological energy and discharge of dammed-up sexual excitation through involuntary contractions of the body (not just the genitals). It excluded the presence of any trace of sadism in the male or masochism in the female, or any sense of prowess or smugness in the male. Furthermore, the surrender is silent, or nearly so. Orgastically potent individuals never talk or laugh during the sexual act—with the exception of uttering words of tenderness. Both talking and laughing indicate a serious lack of the capacity for surrender, which requires an undivided absorption in the sensations of pleasure. Men to whom surrender means being "feminine" are always orgastically "disturbed."

With such high criteria in mind Reich was surely right in asserting that no neurotics are orgastically potent and that the great majority of human beings suffer from a character neurosis. His theories of character armor and orgasm constitute, therefore, a sweeping indictment of the sexual life of civilized man, an indictment similar in many ways to that made by D. H. Lawrence, whom indeed he resembled in combining an intense, almost mystical belief in the prime importance of sex with a puritanical insistence that it should always be treated with high if not dead seriousness. He and Lawrence also had in common the conviction that orgastic potency is a virtue to be found more commonly among working-class men than among aristocrats, bourgeois, and intellectuals, an idea for which no evidence exists.[7]

In working out his theory of the function of the orgasm in preserving and maintaining health, Reich was led to make a minute analysis of the "orgastically satisfying sexual act." This is described, complete with a graph, in Chapter IV, Section 3, of the 1942 version of *The Function of the Orgasm*—which was written after he had persuaded himself that libido (bio-energy) is a "tangible" substance whose movements in the body can be traced and recorded electrically.

[7] See *The Function of the Orgasm*, p. 171.

Reich's account of the ideal sexual act is remarkable both for its explicitness, which must have required courage in the pre-Kinsey, pre-Masters and Johnson era in which it was written, and for its omission of the one word "love." And yet it is clear that it is love he is talking about. Orgastic potency as formulated by Reich is the capacity to love body and soul, psychosomatically —in Pauline terminology it is a matter of the Body and not only of the Spirit or the Flesh—but at this stage in his development his adherence to the natural-scientific approach prevented his saying so.

Another remarkable feature of this account of the sexual act is Reich's insistence that in genital characters it differs physically as well as psychologically from that experienced by the orgastically immature. Whereas the typical civilized man with his inhibiting character armor only experiences "partial releases of tension which are *similar* to orgasm," the genital character experiences an "ultimate vegetatively involuntary surrender" of which lesser mortals have no inkling. Even if one succeeds in attaching some meaning to this phrase and is prepared to accept the idea that there may exist people, presumably either untreated industrial workers or ex-patients of Reich's, who are familiar with this ultimate vegetatively involuntary surrender, one is still left wondering how Reich knew, from what experiences of his own or his patients he derived this insight—or even more how he reached by natural-scientific means the conclusion that "all feelings about nature derive from this function or from the longing for it."

Reich's conviction that all neurotics and indeed most civilized men and women lack full orgastic potency, coupled with his belief in the existence of sexual energies requiring recurrent orgastic discharge, raised for him the question of what happened to these energies when they were not effectively discharged. One answer was, as already mentioned, that they were expended in neurotic symptoms and systems of thought, and provided the energy which activated and maintained infantile sexual phantasies. Another answer was that they were experienced as anxiety. Undischarged energy, which would have been experienced as pleasure if it had been discharged orgastically, is experienced as anxiety if it is discharged through other bodily systems. Here again Reich was following a line of thought begun by Freud, whose original theory of anxiety was that undischarged libido is "converted" into anxiety. This theory, which Freud himself abandoned in the 1920s, assumed that anxiety is a direct physiological result of repressed sexual tension, but the precise nature of the process designated "conversion" was admitted to be mysterious. Reich, in line with his general tendency to remain loyal to Freud's early ideas and to reject his later reformulations, sought to retain Freud's idea of the intimate physiological connection between libido and anxiety by solving the mystery of conversion. This he did by maintaining that anxiety is simply libidinal discharge occurring through the cardiovascular system. Whereas sexual pleasure is experienced in the genitals, anxiety is experienced in the cardiac and diaphragmatic region.[8]

Reich's third answer to the question of the fate of undischarged libido was that it was transformed into

[8] *Ibid.*, p. 110.

sadism; the repressed wish for true orgasm continues to strive for discharge, and the resulting aggression, which in healthy persons is only a means to an end, becomes an end in itself. Love turns into hate, aggression into sadism, all destructive activity being the organism's re-action to the frustration of vital needs.[9]

This view of sadism forms the basis and rationale for the contemporary slogan Make Love Not War, which contains Reich in a nutshell. It appeals immediately to all that is warm, generous, and spontaneous in human nature. It assumes an extraordinarily direct and simple connection between orgastic deprivation and destructive-ness—according to Reich, even genital characters be-come sadists if confronted with a sudden obstacle to their accustomed gratification. And yet it is naïve by its omissions. Just as Reich's confident assertions about the natural placidity and peacefulness of bulls and dogs completely ignore the aggressiveness associated with territoriality (see the writings of Lorenz, Storr, and Ardrey) and the establishment of hierarchical "pecking orders" within animal communities, so the Make Love Not War philosophy completely ignores the psychology of power—and in practical terms such complications as the fact that those who decide to make wars are not, under modern conditions, the people who fight in them and that there is no evidence that the majority of those who do the fighting get any sadistic gratification out of it.

Finally, it must be emphasized that all Reich's ideas about the effects of orgastic frustration derive from

[9] *Ibid.*, p. 132.

psychoanalytical ways of thinking—and were in his own view a defense of Freud's original position against a retrogressive development in psychoanalysis emanating from Freud himself. In the mid-1920s both Freud and Reich, presumably for the same social and historical reasons, became impressed by man's tendency to behave destructively, but whereas Freud sought to explain this by postulating a death instinct, an innate drive toward destructiveness and self-destruction, Reich adopted the explanation that it was due to a much greater and more widespread repression of sexuality than Freud had ever envisaged. And in taking up this position Reich conceived himself to be defending Freud's original revolutionary insights against a loss of nerve and hope on Freud's part.

Both explanations, however, raised as many problems as they solved. Freud's raised problems about the evolutionary status of an instinct that appeared to run counter to evolution, while Reich's raised problems about the origin of man's tendency to construct a character armor against his own nature. Freud's biological justification of the death-instinct concept is singularly unconvincing, since, as Jones, a loyal Freudian if ever there was one, says, "No biological observation can be found to support the idea of a death instinct, one which contradicts all biological principles," and it has been accepted by only a minority even of psychoanalysts. It has, however, contributed to the widespread belief that psychoanalysis is the modern dismal science that sets limits on human progress. Reich, as we shall see, produced at different phases of his life two different and incompatible explanations of the origin of the tendency to construct character armor, the first sociological and the second "religious." Both are still with us; the second indeed always has been, since it resembles closely the account of the Fall of Man given in Genesis.

Reich and the Sexual Paradise

111

Reich's conviction of the prime importance of orgasm in maintaining health, both mental and physical, and in preventing neurosis, led him to formulate a theory of sex economy that contains within itself both a theory of psychopathology and a critique of capitalist society. These are, however, incomprehensible unless one realizes that for Reich the concept of orgasm embraced all that is joyous and spontaneous. His conviction was, if I understand him rightly, that life could be freer and more untrammeled than civilized societies allow it to be, and that if man could live by his instincts and not in submission to his character armor not only would life be freer and richer than it is but also many moral problems and indeed many physical illnesses including cancer would never occur. He seems, indeed, to have believed that suffering is in principle unnecessary, an artifact produced by social restrictions imposed on the life and the wisdom of the body. It is characteristic of his approach that his writings never touch on such awkward problems for the utopian as the inevitability of aging or man's awareness of his mortality. As a result his philosophy of life contained no place for the need for consolation which so many religions claim to supply, nor for the search for meaning. Orgasm and other spontaneous activities were in Reich's view good and meaningful in themselves, and required neither justification nor explanation. Nor, until quite late in his life, does he appear to have considered the possibility that man's self-awareness and capacity to reflect upon his nature and destiny might inherently impair or even modify his capacity for direct animal, childlike enjoyment of living. It is not surprising that from early on in his career he refused to accept theological students and clergymen as patients.

However, Reich, despite his utopian vision of an orgastic, prelapsarian paradise, was also a practical man, and his writings, particularly *The Function of the Orgasm* and *The Sexual Revolution*, contain specific recommendations for reforms that would increase the incidence of sexual happiness and reduce that of neurosis.

These reforms are derived and justified by Reich from his theory of sex economy, which constitutes the core of his thinking. Since, as I know from personal experience, Reich's present followers are all too ready to accuse anyone who writes about him of at the least misrepresenting him and at the worst vilifying him, I shall present this central part of Reich's thinking by quotation from his introduction to the 1942 version of *The Function of the Orgasm*, where he affirms that "the theory of sex-economy can be put in a few sentences." In fact it takes him three pages. In the following numbered paragraphs I quote the main points of his argument.

1. Psychic health depends on orgastic potency.

2. Mental illness is a result of a disturbance in the natural capacity for love.

3. Psychic disturbances are the results of the sexual chaos brought about by the nature of our society. This chaos has, for thousands of years, served the function . . . of internalizing the external mechanization of life . . . bringing about the *psychic anchoring* of a mechanized and authoritarian civilization by way of making people lack self-confidence.

4. The vital energies, under natural conditions, regulate themselves spontaneously.

5. The individual brought up in an atmosphere which negates life and sex acquires a *pleasure-anxiety* (fear of pleasurable excitation) which is represented physiologically in chronic muscular spasms.

6. The character structure of man today—who is perpetuating a patriarchal, authoritarian culture some four to six thousand years old—is characterized by *an armoring against nature within himself and against social misery outside himself*. This armoring of the character is the basis of loneliness, helplessness, craving for authority, fear of responsibility, mystical longing, sexual misery, of impotent rebelliousness as well as of resignation of an unnatural and pathological type.

7. Since [the development of the patriarchal social order] duty has taken the place of the natural enjoyment of work and activity.

8. This formation of character in the authoritarian mold has as its central point, not parental love, but *the authoritarian family*. Its chief instrument is the suppression of sexuality in the infant and the adolescent.

9. Owing to the split in the human structure of today, nature and culture, instinct and morality, sexuality and achievement, are considered incompatible. That *unity of culture and nature, work and love, morality and sexuality* for which mankind is forever longing, this unity will remain a dream as long as man does not permit the satisfaction of the biological demands of natural (orgastic) sexual gratification.[1]

Although Reich's translators must presumably be held responsible for the shaky grammar and the erratic punctuation, these passages illustrate vividly two stylistic peculiarities of his writing, his repetitiveness and his inability to state precisely what he means. In sentences such as "This formation of character in the authoritarian mold has as its central point, not parental love, but the authoritarian family," the general drift of his argument is clear—he is asserting that a particular "authoritarian" mode of behavior on the part of parents tends to produce a particular submissive, inhibited kind of character in their children—but his way of saying this is impressionistic and imprecise; it doesn't really make sense to say that a family can be a central point of a formation of character.

[1] *The Function of the Orgasm*, pp. xviii–xx.

Reich's repetitiveness is, I think, a manifestation of a curious hectoring quality in his character that must have antagonized those who were not hypnotized by it. I, Wilhelm Reich, he seems to be saying, know the truth; and you, reader, have got to believe me and I'm going to go on telling you until you do. This note of strident, dogmatic assertiveness is unfortunately, but surely not accidentally, most apparent in his political writings when he is attacking fascism.

Despite the repetitiveness and imprecision of Reich's own account, his theory of sex economy is in fact capable of perfectly rational formulation. It is a theory that could be true, even if in fact it happens not to be. It can, I think, be summarized in seven propositions:

1. Mental health is dependent on the capacity to experience orgasm in Reich's psychosomatic meaning of the term.

2. Mental illness is the result of inhibition of the capacity to experience orgasm.

3. Inhibition of orgastic capacity is instituted and maintained by a defensive psychological structure, character armor.

4. Character armor is represented physiologically by muscular tension and disturbances of posture.

5. Character armor develops within the individual in response to external pressures antagonistic to sexual expression.

6. These antisexual pressures arise within a specific form of family, the "authoritarian family," which is held together not by parental love but by the oppressive and repressive use of power by the father.

7. This form of family only occurs in patriarchal

societies and is one of the techniques devised by such societies to produce a submissive population incapable of rebelling against its rulers.

The first of these propositions—that, in Reich's own words, "psychic health depends on orgastic potency"—is presented by him as a clinical fact, deriving its authority from the psychoanalytical observations of himself and other analysts. It is, however, open to two methodological objections: that it is tautological, and that it is formulated in a way that makes it impossible to say which comes first, the egg of orgastic potency or the chicken of mental health.

It is, of course, possible to define mental health in a way that designates as ill all persons who lack orgastic potency, and since Freud there has undoubtedly been a widespread tendency to do so, but such a procedure really begs the question, which is after all whether it is indeed a fact that all persons who feel well and whole —and who impress others as being so—possess orgastic potency, and that all persons who suffer mentally and seek psychiatric aid, lack it. Anyone who asserts, as Reich did, an exact correlation between health and orgastic capacity is under an obligation to demonstrate both that all apparently well-adjusted, healthy celibates prove on close investigation to be ill in some definable sense and that the orgastic capacity claimed by, for instance, some schizophrenics and manics is spurious. Reich fails to produce evidence bearing on either point.

Reich's assertion that mental health "depends" on orgastic capacity also begs the question. Even if one agrees that there is some connection between the two, it by no means follows that the former depends on the latter. There are, after all, two other possibilities: that orgastic capacity depends on mental health, and that both are dependent on something else. This latter is, indeed, what Reich the scientist, as opposed to Reich the apostle of the orgasm, really thought. He held that there are two necessary preconditions for the development and maintenance of both mental health and orgastic potency: a childhood spent in a family in which infantile sexuality is not suppressed, and an adulthood spent in a society in which sexual activity is not restricted by religious taboos or economic restraints.

The second proposition—that, again in Reich's own words, "mental illness is a result of a disturbance in the natural capacity for love"—is quite simply untrue. Although some mental illnesses, notably the psychoneuroses and the sexual perversions, have arguably and indeed probably some connection with disturbances in the natural capacity for love, others quite certainly have not. It is characteristic of Reich's utopianism and predilection for sweeping generalizations that he discusses mental illness as though he had never heard of mental deficiency or of organic mental illnesses caused by brain damage, metabolic disorders, senility, heredity, etc. And yet as a doctor and psychiatrist he must have been familiar with these illnesses, and have known that there is no way in which even the most ingenious intellect could make out a case for their being even remote results of a disturbance in the natural capacity for love.

In view of my earlier account of character armor and its relation to the psychoanalytical concept "defense," it is unnecessary for me to discuss it further here, except perhaps to add that one of the problems created by the idea of a ubiquitous character armor imprisoning civilized man is that of deciding which aspects of human culture are manifestations of the armor and which are expressions of those aspects of the natural man that succeed in surviving or transcending the armor. It is clear that in Reich's view all actions based on a sense of duty stem from the armor and that all actions based on a sense of compassion stem from the natural man, but it is much less clear to what extent he would have agreed with Marcuse, another post-Freudian Marxist utopian, that much of bourgeois culture is "affirmative," in the sense of providing an area of experience in which man's "longing for a happier life; for humanity, goodness, joy, truth and solidarity,"[2] can be realized without threatening the taboos and restrictions of capitalist society. Marcuse's view, expressed in his *Eros and Civilization*, is that Reich failed to make any essential distinction between repressive and non-repressive sublimation and that his sociological insights are vitiated by a "sweeping primitivism": "progress in freedom appears as a mere release in sexuality." In fact, Reich's attitude to culture seems to have been simple-minded rather than primitive. In his view sexual satisfaction was a prerequisite of cultural and creative activity. "The few bad poems which occasionally are created during abstinence are of no great interest."[3]

Reich's fourth idea—that character armor is represented by and indeed in some sense identical with chronic muscular tensions—will be discussed later, in

[2] Herbert Marcuse, "The Affirmative Character of Culture," in his *Negations* (Boston: Beacon Press, 1968).
[3] *The Sexual Revolution*, p. 66.

the chapter on vegetotherapy, since it was this observation, hypothesis, or insight which led Reich to abandon psychoanalysis and to experiment with physical forms of treatment.

The fifth proposition—that character armor is the result of internalization of external pressures imposed by society and the family on individuals who under natural conditions would grow up healthy and sexually free—has already been discussed. But it is perhaps worth emphasizing that it constituted a major break with two of Freud's ideas: that of the death instinct, which postulates the existence of an innate tendency in man toward morbidity; and that of the inherent weakness of the child's ego, which compels it to construct defenses for its own sake to protect itself from being overwhelmed by its own excessive instinctual impulses. As we shall see, Reich abandoned this environmental, sociological theory of the origin of character armor during his later "religious" phase—without, however, in any way reverting to Freud's position.

The first point to be made about Reich's sixth argument—that character armor arises only within a specific authoritarian type of family—is that it is a sociological or ideological concept, not a clinical finding. Reich is not maintaining that his psychoanalytical experience has led him to postulate a correlation between family structure and the neuroses of the constituent family members, or that all his cases displaying character armor grew up in authoritarian families, in which the fathers oppressed their wives and children and repressed all manifestations of infantile sexuality. If he had, it would be possible to claim him as a pioneer of contemporary family psychiatry and to argue that he anticipated some of the findings that have been made by applying Gregory Bateson's "double bind" theory of schizophrenia to families containing neurotic and psychotic members.

For it does indeed seem to be true that there are families that are held together not by parental love but by the exercise of power, and that such families produce neurotic and psychotic children in significant numbers. But it seems not to be true that in these families the pathogenic power is necessarily exercised by the father —indeed, the literature contains many more references to dominating "schizophrenogenic" and "neurotogenic" mothers with weak husbands than to authoritarian fathers—or that repression of infantile sexuality is the only or even the main technique by which such parents exert power over their children, forcing them into neurotic submissiveness; indulgence, overprotectiveness, and seductiveness seem to be just as efficient destructive weapons. Nor of course do appearances and realities necessarily coincide; a family can appear to be ruled by an authoritarian father when in fact it is dominated by a mother who prefers to rule from behind the throne.

However, Reich's idea that character armor, and hence neurosis, was the result of internalization of the repressive, antilibidinal values of the authoritarian family was not derived from clinical observation, nor indeed was it adduced to explain clinical phenomena. It was introduced for two quite different reasons: to reconcile psychoanalysis and Marxism, and to eliminate a discrepancy in Marxist theory.

It was Reich's contention that the oppression of the

masses by the ruling classes could not be explained by orthodox Marxist theory, simply in terms of the material power wielded by the latter; the ruling classes were in his view only successful in controlling the masses because bourgeois society creates people with a character structure that renders them submissive toward authority and willing to be ruled by their rulers. It was not that society was the result of a certain psychic structure, but that character structure was the result of a certain society. Furthermore, bourgeois society produces the character structure it requires through the mediation of various social institutions, notably the authoritarian family, the authoritarian school, and religion. As a result, the character structure of the majority "corresponds to the interests of the political and economic rulers."[4]

This formulation of the relationship between the structure of society, the structure of the family, and the character of the individual, had the merit of solving, to Reich's satisfaction at least, unresolved problems in both psychoanalysis and Marxism. It provided an explanation of the origin of neurosis without recourse to fanciful biological theories such as the death instinct, and it resolved the discrepancy in Marxist theory created by the fact, which was all too obvious during the rise of fascism, that the masses do not pursue the real economic interests of their own class but are instead only too willing to follow authoritarian leaders.

It is not at all clear how Reich arrived at his idea that character structure, family structure, and social struc-

---

[4] *The Sexual Revolution,* p. xx.

ture are functionally correlated—"functionally identical" in his own terminology—but it can be seen as an example of his consistent application of what is nowadays usually called holistic thinking, which starts from the assumption that phenomena, including persons, are not discrete entities, complete and comprehensible in themselves—"no man is an island, entire of itself"— but are parts of larger wholes. Just as Arthur Koestler (who incidentally was in the same Communist party cell as Reich in Berlin) postulates in *The Ghost in the Machine* that all phenomena can be arranged in a hierarchy of holons (e.g., electrons, atoms, molecules, cells, organs, organisms, etc.), each of which can be regarded both as an entity in itself and as part of a larger, more complex controlling superentity, so Reich thought of neurotic symptoms as part of a neurotic structure, which was itself part of a character structure, which was part of a family structure, which was part of a social structure, etc., the larger structure being socially or psychologically represented within its smaller component units.

Although, as Robinson points out, Reich's social theory "offers an imaginative conceptual tool for sociological and historical research," which could be used "to understand how economic realities are translated into politics, ethics and religion, indeed even to understand how the economic order itself is maintained," Reich in fact never worked it out in a way that was academically acceptable. "The crude, undisciplined character of his mind did not lend itself to a patient empirical elaboration of his basic insight. In this respect, as in so many others, he fell short of the greatest social theorists, who never considered scholarly historical research beneath their dignity."[5]

Incidentally, Reich's theory of orgasm is itself an example of holistic thinking, since it asserts simultaneously that orgasms are necessary for the physical and mental health of the individual considered as a single entity and that to fulfill this function orgasms must be in partnership with someone else. The need for orgastic experience is therefore the crucial biological evidence that human adults are not autonomous, self-sufficient units who happen at times to relate to one another but are intrinsically members one of another. Reich was always insistent that masturbation is an inherently unsatisfying and tantalizing experience; "in the long run it becomes unsatisfactory and quite disturbing because soon the lack of a love object becomes painful."[6]

Although some of Reich's followers, notably the editors of *Reich Speaks of Freud*, have played down Reich's involvement with Communism and Marxism, even to the extent of claiming that it arose solely out of his interest in sexual hygiene, there can be no doubt that he was deeply committed to Communism for several years. Although there are understandable reasons of political expediency for soft-pedaling the fact, he belonged to a generation of the intelligentsia, most of whose members were sympathetic toward Communism. In the late 1920s and early 1930s it was not yet obvious that

[5] Paul A. Robinson, *The Freudian Left* (New York: Harper & Row, 1969), p. 45.
[6] *The Sexual Revolution*, p. 110.

Leninism was turning into Stalinism or that the Soviet Union was going to emerge as yet another imperialist power.

One of the difficulties of the Marxist position in general and of Reich's version of it in particular is that of knowing how much reality can be attached to its widest abstractions. It is not hard to attach meaning to concepts such as "character structure," "the family," authoritarian or otherwise, "the state," "class," but it is much less easy to be sure that there is such an entity as "bourgeois society," or to know what social or historical phenomena are legitimately embraced by such a concept as the "patriarchal authoritarian culture" which, according to Reich, has been in existence for the last four to six thousand years. This is indeed one of Reich's most peculiar ideas and it will require a brief excursus into the history of anthropology if we are to understand how he came to entertain it.

According to Reich's theory of the origin of contemporary society and its neuroses, the original "natural" society was matriarchal. Politically, this society lacked any system of domination; sexually, it was entirely permissive. Since fathers had no power, children had no Oedipus complex, repression did not occur, and everyone was happy, free, and spontaneous. Although this idea is patently a fantasy, Reich seems really to have believed that such an idyllic state of affairs did once exist. "In primitive society, which has a collective and work-democratic organization, the unit is the clan, comprising all the blood relatives of a common mother. Within this clan, which is also the economic unit, there is no other

marriage than the loose ties of a sexual relationship."
However, as a result of unexplained economic changes,
matriarchy is gradually replaced by patriarchy, and

> "natural" sexual sociality is replaced by the demands
> of morality; voluntary, happy, love relationship is
> replaced by "marital duty". . . . Sex-economically
> regulated life is replaced by genital repression,
> neurotic disturbances and sexual perversions; the
> naturally strong, self-reliant biological organism be-
> comes weak, helpless, dependent, fearful of God; the
> orgastic experiencing of nature is replaced by mystical
> ecstasy.[7]

One has only to ask where this matriarchal society
was, when it existed, and what records of it survive to
realize that this is anthropological fantasy, bearing no
relation to historical reality. But to be fair to Reich, it
is no more a fantasy than is Freud's account in *Totem
and Taboo* of the origin of the Oedipus complex and of
neurotic guilt in the murder of the Primal Father by his
rebellious sons. And to be fair to both of them, it must
be added that they were both engaging in a form of
speculative activity that was accepted as legitimate at
the time but that has been invalidated by subsequent
developments in anthropology. They were in fact constructing fantasies based on two assumptions that were
accepted by the majority of nineteenth-century anthropologists but that are rejected by all contemporary ones,
whether functional or structural.

The first assumption is that the concept of evolution
can be applied directly to human societies. This idea,

[7] *Ibid.*, pp. 161–62.

which derives from Spencer, leads to further subassumptions that some societies are "primitive" and others evolved or "advanced," and that existing "primitive" societies provide evidence of what advanced societies were like before they evolved. The analogy is, of course, with biology. The fact that fishes, amphibia, reptiles, and mammals can be arranged in an evolutionary series, "the diapason closing full in man," and that there are still fishes, reptiles, etc., alive in a world apparently dominated by man, was used to justify the idea that "primitive," i.e., non-European societies, were survivals from earlier phases in the evolution of "civilized," i.e., European, man. Furthermore, since many of these so-called primitive societies hold beliefs that strike Western intellectuals as irrational and illogical, attempts were made to explain these as early evolutionary stages in the development of the capacity for logical and rational thinking. And on the basis of the biological law that ontogeny recapitulates phylogeny, parallels were drawn between the minds of savages and those of European, usually middle-class, children. As Roger S. Poole puts it:

> It was a question of fitting together savage fancy with civilized fact, and no one at the time seemed even the slightest bit embarrassed by this appalling presumption. Progressivist and evolutionist superiority then, the belief in the linear advance of civilization, the belief in the search for origins, the assumption that all logics should operate according to the same axes of signification, such was the picture of nineteenth-century and some twentieth-century speculation.[8]

[8] Roger S. Poole, Introduction to Claude Lévi-Strauss, *Totemism* (London: Penguin, 1969), p. 15.

The second assumption made both by Freud, when he traced the origins of the Oedipus complex back to a primal, patriarchal horde, and by Reich, when he asserted that the earliest human society was matriarchal, was that the conventions governing kinship and the tracing of lineages reflect the structure of a society and the nature of the power relationships existing within it. According to this assumption, the fact that, as was originally believed, all "primitive" societies are patrilineal, i.e., trace lineages and define kinship relationships through the male line, was regarded as valid evidence that all societies are ruled by men and that this had always been so.

However, this rather simple view of the matter did not survive detailed and systematic investigation of specific societies made by anthropologists who actually went to live in them, instead of just staying, as for instance Frazer did, in their studies collating evidence derived from travelers' tales. It then turned out not only that kinship rules and social structures were much more varied and complicated than had previously been realized, and that societies which resembled one another in being in the widest sense patrilineal might have very different social organizations, but also that some societies were matrilineal, tracing lineage and kinship primarily through the female line.

It was this latter fact that Reich seized upon to construct his theory that natural, primitive society is matriarchal. Following Bachofen, Morgan, and Engels, he assumed that matrilineal societies were matriarchal, and argued that they represented survivals from an earlier stage of human evolutionary development corresponding to Marx's era of primitive communism, in which there had been no state, no private property, and no sexual repression.

In support of this thesis Reich made considerable use of Malinowski's studies of the Trobriand islanders of Melanesia. Among the Trobriand islanders descent is matrilineal, physiological paternity is not acknowledged, and there are no social restraints imposed upon the sexual activities of either children or adolescents and adults prior to marriage. They seemed indeed to have no Oedipus complex, no sexual repressions, and to provide convincing evidence with which to refute Freud's pessimistic view that guilt and repression were the result of an innate, phylogenetically determined Oedipus complex and therefore inescapable aspects of the human condition. As a result Reich cited Malinowski's work in support of his contention that "savages" show a far superior sex economy[9] and used the idea that there exist sexually permissive, primitive matriarchal societies to support his thesis that his sexual paradise was practical politics. It already existed in Melanesia, it had occurred in pre-history; it could therefore be introduced into "advanced" societies after the Sexual Revolution.

Reich was, however, wrong on one essential point. Although the Trobriand islanders are matrilineal, their society is not matriarchal and Malinowski himself never suggested that it was. Nor did he use his researches to support evolutionary speculations about the original nature of human society. Indeed, as a functional anthropologist he did not consider such speculations

[9] See *The Sexual Revolution*, p. 131.

legitimate. In his view the customs and beliefs of the Trobriand islanders needed to be explained in terms of their function within the totality of their culture, not in terms of any social-evolutionary theory. So in using Malinowski's evidence to construct a theory about the nature of natural, primitive society, Reich was misunderstanding Malinowski's work and being old-fashioned into the bargain. Reich's misuse of Malinowski's researches is indeed an excellent example of how he looked for data to support theses, instead of constructing theories to explain facts.

In fact power in matrilineal societies still resides with the men, and men still exert authority over children. Malinowski himself described the frictions that arise between Trobriand fathers and their brothers-in-law over the discipline and future careers of their son-nephews, and there seems to be no doubt that the whole idea of matriarchy is a myth. As Robin Fox puts it: "The whole problem with matrilineal systems [is] how to combine continuity and recruitment through females with control by the *men* of the lineage." Fox goes on to point out that for most men the idea of matriarchy conjures up an Amazonian world in which

> men would be of no account and would be used for breeding purposes only. Such a sinister practice exists only in the imagination, although most people have at some time or another accused their neighbors of it, or at least of being in some way "matriarchal." Thus Athens accused Sparta, France accused England, and now we are accusing the Americans. It probably arises from a deep-rooted fear on the part of men that they will lose their position, and the fear is projected onto disliked nations. Be this as it may, the true Ama-

zonian solution is unknown. Women don't ever seem to have got quite such a grip on things.[10]

Reich was therefore most unusual in idealizing matriarchy and in conceiving of women solely as sources of love and not at all as threatening dominators. His whole political, social, and sexual stance can indeed be interpreted as a massive rejection or dismissal of the problem of dominance in human relationships. It was possible, he believed, to conceive of a world in which nobody dominated anyone in any way whatsover. One again wonders what he would have made of the recent ethological work which suggests that the establishment of hierarchies, in which each member of a group has and knows his place, is one of the basic biological mechanisms for maintaining peace and cohesion within groups. It appears, however, that the impulse to dominate was clearly visible in Reich's own character.

[10] Robin Fox, *Kinship and Marriage* (London: Penguin, 1967), p. 113.

The Sexual Revolution

IV

In the previous chapter I remarked that Reich was a practical man, and it is a striking fact that many of the specific reforms he recommended in *The Function of the Orgasm* and *The Sexual Revolution* are perfectly sensible and reasonable, and can often be justified on simple grounds of humanity without needing the support of theoretical and ideological constructions. In particular, he displays great understanding of the crippling effects of poverty and lack of privacy on human relationships.

However, Reich was a typical central European intellectual in believing that no idea was satisfactorily stated until it had been underpinned by an impressive theoretical substructure and been clearly placed in its appropriate position in a completely formulated *Weltanschauung*.

Furthermore, as a doctor and an adherent to Freud's idea that psychology should be based on the natural sciences, he believed that all propositions about human nature should be formulated in terms that at least sound scientific. As a result all the reforms proposed by Reich to bring about his Sexual Revolution are presented, scientifically, as logical deductions from his theory of sex economy and, medically, as prophylactic measures for the prevention of neurosis.

Since, according to Reich, "the plague of the neuroses is bred during three principal phases of life," childhood, puberty, and adulthood, his proposals are best considered under these three headings.

In Reich's view the two factors in childhood most productive of neurosis were strict and premature toilet-training and the prohibition of childhood masturbation. Although Reich, with his sexological bias, can hardly be said to have emphasized the point, he nonetheless consistently held that strict toilet-training is harmful. In doing so he was affirming an idea generally accepted in the psychoanalytical circles of his time. As I mentioned earlier, the idea that "character" could be a defense first arose in psychoanalysis in connection with anal erotism, the development of the obsessional character with its triad of compulsive obstinacy, orderliness, and parsimony being attributed to severe and early toilet-training. A case could be made out for maintaining that the whole of Reich's work on character armor is really a study of the pervasive individual and social effects of obsessional defenses. Many analysts who are totally uninfluenced by Reich are ready to agree that bourgeois society is basically obsessional, though not all of them would go on to argue that this is necessarily a bad thing. The issue raised by Reich as to whether human beings can do without character armor or obsessional defenses, and can rely instead on an inherent tendency to self-regulation, is by no means dead in psychoanalytical circles, and has recently been raised again, though in less specifically sexual or anal terms by both Laing and Winnicott in their writings on the true and false self.

Here it must be mentioned that, psychoanalytically speaking, Reich was very much a child of his own times in not discussing the role of the early oral attachment to the mother in the causation of neurosis. Psychoanalysis only became interested in the first year of life after Reich had ceased to be connected with it, and the pioneers in this field, Melanie Klein and Winnicott, worked in London, not in Vienna. Since contemporary research into the infant's early relationship with its mother has led to increasing awareness of the importance of grief, depression, and despair in both normal and neurotic development, Reich's remarkable obliviousness to this aspect of human experience, which shows up perhaps most noticeably in his habit of discussing sexual relationships without mentioning the grief and sense of loss which attends their termination, can be interpreted historically as a reflection of the state of psychoanalysis in Vienna in the 1920s. It is, however, impossible not to wonder whether it was also part of his own personal need to deny the implications of the premature deaths of his own parents.

However, despite Reich's failure to consider the possible role of disturbances in the original mother-

infant relationship in breeding neurosis, it can be sur-
mised with some confidence that his antiauthoritarian
attitude would have led him to disapprove of feeding by
the clock, that his belief in spontaneity in all things
would have made him an advocate of demand feeding,
and that his faith in instinct would have made him a
believer in close and continuous physical intimacy between mothers and their infants.

Reich's objection to the prohibition of infantile
masturbation arose primarily from his conviction that
inhibition of infantile sexuality was the basis for the
fixation to the "family" and was the origin of a
"typical" lack of independence in thought and action.[1]

However, despite his conviction that suppression of
infantile sexuality was the main source of Western
man's submissiveness and lack of spontaneity, he did
not hold that all infantile masturbation is in fact healthy
and spontaneous. On the contrary, he seems to have
been one of the first psychoanalysts to appreciate how
often it is a compulsive symptom and is engendered by
conflict and not by desire. In *The Sexual Revolution*[2] he
quotes with approval the observation of the Russian
psychoanalyst Vera Schmitt, who ran a children's home
in Moscow in the early 1920s, that there are two forms
of childhood masturbation; one which is spontaneous
and genuinely erotic, and another which is a response to
insult, disparagement, or limitation of freedom. Reich's
recognition of the importance of this distinction goes
hand in hand with his insistence that much of what

[1] See *The Function of the Orgasm*, pp. 171–72.
[2] See p. 245.

passes for normal sexual activity among European adults is really a compulsive neurotic symptom, impelled by anxiety and sadism, not by genuine sexual desire.

Reich's views on puberty as a phase of life during which neuroses are created were based on the simple and straightforward premise that *"puberty signifies coming into sexual maturity,* and primarily nothing else."[3] Since according to sex-economic principles sexual abstinence produces sexual stasis, and sexual stasis reactivates infantile neurotic patterns of behavior, Reich advocated complete sexual freedom for all young persons above the age of fifteen. In his view the prohibitions and restraints imposed on the sexual activities of adolescents not only caused an enormous amount of frustration and misery at the time, but also had permanent and crippling effects on the personality; these crippling effects being indeed the reason why the prohibitions were imposed. Their social function was to make each new generation submissive and conformist and, in particular, sufficiently inhibited to accept meekly the limitations on orgastic satisfaction imposed by the institution of monogamous "compulsive marriage"; while the motive underlying the imposition was "fear of youth's sexuality and fighting spirit."[4]

Reich's analysis of the problem of puberty in Chapter VI of *The Sexual Revolution* is a vivid and in many ways understanding account of the predicament of sexually awakened young people growing up in a culture that demands sexual abstinence for several years after puberty. Too much of it is as applicable today as it was

[3] The Function of the Orgasm, p. 173. Reich's italics.
[4] *Ibid.,* p. 173.

in 1930, when the original German version was published. Indeed, if it were true that "puberty signifies coming into sexual maturity, *and primarily nothing else*" (my italics this time), Reich's position would be unassailable. But in fact and as usual Reich's whole method of argument begs all the difficult questions—this time in two different ways.

First, even if it were true that sexual misery was unknown in his much beloved primitive matriarchal societies, the onus is really on Reich to show that this freedom from sexual misery is not purchased at a price, i.e., to demonstrate that there is no functional connection or correlation between the development of the hygienic, cultural, and aesthetic amenities of literate and technologically advanced civilizations and the postponement for educational purposes of adult status for some years after puberty. Any thorough comparison of the degrees of sexual happiness or misery experienced by members of different cultures would have to take into account the relationship of their sexual customs to all other nonsexual aspects of the cultures, including both the availability or otherwise of other forms of satisfaction and the average duration of life. Perhaps Melanesians do enjoy an adolescence without sexual frustration and misery, but I doubt whether they live as long as we do.

There is also the question of the quality of love, and in particular of the romantic ideal of "falling in love," which our society values highly (though perhaps decreasingly so), but which is rare elsewhere and is generally regarded outside Western Europe and North

America as a socially disruptive phenomenon.[5] When one considers the amount of intense happiness and misery experienced by young people who fall in love, one realizes that it would require a more subtle exponent of hedonic calculus than Reich to decide whether his sort of sexual freedom would increase or decrease the total sum of human happiness. Reich, however, blocks all discussion of these real and still-open issues by his blanket assumption that all sexual repression is a technique of social oppression.

The second way in which Reich begs the question is by making the a priori assumption that all adolescents who do not actively seek sexual intercourse the moment they reach puberty are neurotic. This assumption enables him to use apparent evidence against his thesis as evidence for it, without having to prove that he is entitled to do so. In Reich's view all teen-agers who do not have sexual intercourse from the age of fifteen onward refrain from doing so out of fear of their parents and are submissive persons, without ambition.[6] I doubt whether this is true; some are just not ready for it. It seems to be a characteristic of our culture that psychological and emotional development often lags behind physical maturation, so that sexual awakening often occurs an appreciable time after puberty. To assume, as Reich does, that this lag is necessarily a symptom of neurosis seems to me to be a typical Reichian oversimplification and abuse of psychopathology. It involves

[5] See Geoffrey Gorer's essay "On Falling in Love," in his *The Danger of Equality* (New York: Weybright and Talley, 1968).
[6] See *The Sexual Revolution*, p. 83.

the same fallacy as the "crude" Marxist idea that artistic and cultural movements are mere epiphenomenal reflections of economic and class interests without any historical dynamic of their own. It also assumes that orgastic satisfaction is an aim that can be pursued in isolation from all the other needs that draw human beings toward one another.

Reich makes things easy for himself in a number of other ways. He completely ignores friendships between members of the same sex, and indeed everything that can be related to the homosexual component of human nature. This is a remarkable omission when one considers the extent to which the education of adolescents has been, and still largely remains, a process by which knowledge, skills, and cultural attitudes are transmitted from one generation to another by relationships between teachers and pupils of the same sex. He also assumes that contraceptives are always reliable, which they certainly weren't in the 1930s, and as a result he largely ignores all problems related to pregnancy, childbirth, and abortion. Indeed, despite all his sympathy for the young and the sexually frustrated, and despite too his pose of being down to earth, *The Sexual· Revolution* conjures up a bleak and curiously unreal picture of adolescence. In Reich's vision all young people are lonely and longing, none of them has brothers and sisters or friends, and none of them is fond of his parents. The generation gap is always absolute, no parent ever remembering what it was like to be young, and no young person ever enjoying the company of his parents.

In Reich's view the most fertile soil of neurosis in

adulthood was "compulsive marriage," by which he meant conventional, monogamous, "bourgeois" marriage. In his opinion this form of human relationship was emphatically not an expression of any natural need for continuity and permanence in human companionship or for mutual enjoyment of parenthood, but was the result of social, economic and moral pressures, particularly on women, and of indoctrination in childhood.[7] Despite the fact that according to Reich's theories the social function of both repression of infantile sexuality and the restrictions imposed on the sexual life of adolescents was to construct a type of personality that would find compulsive marriage acceptable if not actively enjoyable, his critique of bourgeois marriage is basically that these preparations for it are ineffective. In his view bourgeois marriage founders on an inherent conflict between sexual and economic needs, since the former cannot be satisfied indefinitely without a change of partner, while the latter, which are reinforced by habit and moral pressures, militate toward its continuation.[8]

It must be noted that Reich has here insinuated into his argument a commonly held, but scientifically unproven, assumption about human nature, viz., that both men and women are naturaly polygamous. As a result they inevitably tire of "one and the same partner" after a "limited period of time."

This idea that full sexual capacity and monogamy are incompatible led Reich to speak of an "inherent contradiction in the institution of marriage." In view of

[7] *The Function of the Orgasm*, p. 174.
[8] *Ibid.*, pp. 174–75.

WILHELM REICH | 62

Reich's remarkable sense of certitude about what are, after all, merely his own personal opinions—the mind boggles at the idea of constructing a scientific demonstration that man is naturally polygamous (heterotropic) and that monogamous (monotropic) behavior is pathological, or alternatively that man is naturally monogamous and all polygamous behavior is pathological—it is not surprising that he was even prepared to make a definite statement about the average duration of natural permanent sexual relationships; they last for four years.[9]

Similarly, and equally rashly, Reich commits himself to a definite statement about the orgastic needs of healthy genital characters. They require three to four thousand orgasms in the course of a sexual life lasting thirty to forty years.[10] To save readers the trouble of working out the mathematics of this statement, it means that genital characters average between seventy-five and one hundred thirty-three orgasms a year, figures which are modest by contemporary Kinsey ratings. They also imply, when we bear in mind Reich's view that sexual life begins at fifteen, that orgastic capacity disappears between the ages of forty-five and fifty-five, a curiously Victorian idea to come from a sexual enthusiast. But Reich never seems to have concerned himself with the psychology or sexual physiology of the middle-aged and old.

The sexual revolution envisaged and proclaimed by Reich would consist therefore in the social recognition of the importance and value of the "permanent sexual rela-

[9] *The Sexual Revolution*, pp. 139–40.
[10] *The Function of the Orgasm*, p. 175.

tionship" existing solely for the mutual orgastic gratification of the two partners to it and clearly differentiated from marriage as a social and economic contract. It would indeed amount to a total severance of the historical links between marriage as a legal institution concerned with the support and protection of women and children, and with the inheritance of property, and marriage as a public affirmation of mutual love. As Reich himself saw clearly, such a revolution would presuppose radical changes of both a social and psychological kind.

Socially it presupposes a world in which women are economically independent, either by being able to earn their own livings or by receiving state subsidies for the maintenance of their children, in which fathers play a relatively unimportant role in the lives of their children, and in which crèches and nursery schools are available for the children of working mothers. Psychologically, it demands the elimination of possessiveness in human relationships. In Reich's view jealousy was a natural emotion—"It is absolutely natural to suffer pain at the thought of the beloved partner in somebody else's arms" —but he also believed that it is equally unnatural to seek to prevent a former partner from starting a relationship with someone else. This is another example of Reich's belief that the exercise of power is not an essential aspect of human nature.

Since there are today circles in most metropolitan areas of Western Europe and the United States in which something approximating the sexual revolution has already occurred, and has done so without any accompanying economic revolution, it must be emphasized that Reich formulated his theory of sex economy in the 1930s and that at least three social changes have taken place in the intervening years which neither he nor any of his Marxist contemporaries anticipated. First, capitalism, so far from being in its death throes, has shown itself capable of surviving a world war without radical changes in the distribution of power between classes. Second, in highly industrialized countries capitalism has entered into a phase not predicted by Marx, in which class power is maintained not by force and poverty but by the persuasive powers of the mass media and by the provision of material affluence for the more articulate sections of the population, e.g., salaried workers, the professions, and business executives, who remain nonetheless excluded from real power. As a result the revolutionary impetus resides not, as prewar Marxists believed, in the proletariat and other "progressive elements" of technologically advanced industrial societies but in rural, developing areas such as Africa, Asia, and Latin America. And third, the correlation between class structure and sexual morality has proved, in industrial societies at least, to be less close than Reich believed; permissive sexual morality seems to offer little threat to bourgeois property relationships. The invention and commercial exploitation of reliable contraceptives is a major cause of this last unexpected development.

Finally, it must be added that neuroses and sexual inhibitions (hang-ups) are far from being unknown in circles that distinguish clearly between marriage as a legal institution and "permanent sexual relationships." In such circles the neuroses of frustration have, it seems, been replaced by neuroses of confusion. And the economic independence of the women involved is often not based on their freedom to work and earn money but on alimony or unearned, inherited incomes. Indeed, as many observers have pointed out, the sexual revolution has so far at least proved to be largely an upper-middle-class phenomenon having little if anything to do with the class war.

Vegetotherapy

V

In the previous chapter I mentioned that one of the fundamental principles of Reich's theory of sex economy is the idea that character armor is represented somatically in muscular tensions and various stereotyped postures and gestures; in other words, that character armor is accompanied by or, in Reich's own rather curious terminology, is "functionally identical," with "muscular armor." This idea, hypothesis, or insight—it is difficult to decide which word to use—that the overcontrolled, inhibited, unspontaneous character neurotic is also literally a rigid, tense, unrelaxed person led Reich to make a step in therapy that constituted a final break with psychoanalysis, since it occurred to him that it might be possible to attack the character defense directly through the body. If by appropriate manipulation of his muscular armor the patient was rendered incapable of sustaining his defenses against the spontaneous expression of emotion, these would be released—and the long, arduous, and not always successful psychological techniques of defense and character analysis could be either replaced or supplemented by a direct physical approach to the patient's person.

Although, when expressed in such simple terms, this new therapeutic technique, which Reich called vegetotherapy, sounds in no way startling or outrageous, it constituted a complete break with the psychoanalytical tradition that psychoanalysis is a "talking cure," in which the analyst maintains his physical and psychological distance from the patient, this distancing being justified on two theoretical grounds: that neuroses are psychological illnesses and are therefore only appropriately treated by psychological techniques; and second that the analyst must preserve his anonymity, or rather unactuality, as a person in order to ensure that all the patient's reactions to him can be interpreted as transference phenomena, i.e., as revivals of past feelings of love and hate toward the significant figures in his childhood and not as direct, actual responses to his present therapist's behavior.

There seems to be well-authenticated evidence that this new technique of Reich's was at times highly successful. Both the English educationalist A. S. Neill and the Norwegian psychiatrist Nic Waal vouch for its effectiveness on themselves and on others.[1] Neill writes, "All I need say here about it is that I got more emo-

---

[1] See Paul Ritter, ed., *Wilhelm Reich*.

tional reaction and relief after six weeks of his therapy than I'd had in several years of talkie analysis. It was no picnic; it meant many a painful hour. I was possibly too old to get the full benefit of the treatment, but on the other hand I gained something more important to me— the friendship of a warm, sincere, brilliant man," while Nic Waal, who like Neill had also had previous experience of "talkie analysis," writes:

> He detected at once—quite unlike my previous therapists, that I had used a lively and vital erotism as a defence against aggression and depression. He detected at once also that I had severe problems around aggression, that I was falsely kind and a false "yes-sayer." It was a terrible revelation, but I knew he was right, that what I had fought for theoretically and personally was really a true fight. I could stand being crushed by Reich because I liked truth. And strangely enough, I was not crushed by it. All through this therapeutic attitude to me, he had a loving voice, he sat beside me and made me look at him. He accepted me and crushed only my vanity and falseness. But I understood at that moment that true honesty and love both in a therapist and in parents is sometimes the courage to be seemingly cruel when it is necessary. It demands, however, a great deal of the therapist, his training and his diagnosis of the patient.

However, despite her own enthusiastic and grateful personal response to Reich, Nic Waal goes on to voice her professional misgivings about his very direct approach toward his patients: "I am not sure that Reich really always had the tool at that time to diagnose the patient, when unfolding his cruel and penetrating technique. I do not think he was detached from what happened to him to go through this necessary therapeutic diagnosis toward all those, to whom he gave therapy. Some became either crushed or obsessively oppositional or projective by his active therapy. But many were rescued from severe personality problems."

Both these quotations show that vegetotherapy with Reich was a highly dramatic, direct encounter with Reich's personality, and that its effectiveness depended as much on the patient's capacity to believe that Reich radiated love as on any theories that Reich as a scientist might happen to be holding at the time. And it is at this point in the development of Reich's ideas that his theories begin to become peculiar, to put it mildly. Incidentally, neither Neill nor Nic Waal followed Reich in his later move from vegetotherapy to orgone therapy, although both remained personally loyal and attached to him.

Reich's own account of vegetotherapy is given in Chapter VIII of the 1942 edition of *The Function of the Orgasm.* Contemporary readers, particularly if they are not medically trained, will have difficulties with it, since much of its theoretical formulation is based on a number of assumptions about the nature and function of what in the 1930s and 1940s was commonly known as the vegetative nervous system—i.e., that part of the nervous system which is NOT subject to voluntary control and which innervates those organs, such as the heart, intestines, and genitals, that are not capable of being affected directly by acts of will. This system, which is now usually called the autonomic nervous system, is divided into two parts, the sympathetic and parasympathetic systems, and Reich persuaded himself that it was possible to establish a direct correlation between parasympathetic activity and pleasure on one hand and between sympathetic activity and anxiety on the other. It seems, indeed, that he believed that the unconscious was located in the parasympathetic system, and that this belief satisfied his early expressed wish to find something tangible corresponding to every idea. Vegetotherapy was therefore rationalized theoretically as an attempt to liberate the expansive, pleasure-giving, outgoing, life-enhancing forces contained in the parasympathetic vegetative centers from the restrictive, shrinking, inhibiting effects of sympathetic stimulation. In typical Reichian manner, this presumed antagonism between the two systems was epitomized in slogans: the parasympathetic nervous system stood for "Toward the world, out of the self" and the sympathetic nervous system stood for "Away from the world, back into the self."

However, this vegetative theory need not be taken too seriously, since Reich himself offends against it in two different ways. He frequently uses the word "vegetative" in an entirely arbitrary, private sense of his own to describe "good" ideas such as "natural," "spontaneous," "sexual," quite regardless of the possible neurophysiological processes which may or may not be involved in what he is describing. And much of his actual "vegetotherapy" was concerned with "muscular armor" phenomena occurring in voluntary muscles that are not innervated by the vegetative (autonomic) nervous system at all.

A further difficulty that will disturb all but the most devoted Reichians is that his account of vegetotherapy contains a number of dogmatic, categorical statements of such improbability that one is tempted to dismiss the whole chapter as nonsensical. For instance, he asserts that inhibition of respiration is the basic mechanism of the neurosis in general, and that neurotics use as their primary defense mechanism the technique of reducing their vitality by breathing in less oxygen.[2] An even more preposterous notion is his idea, based on very shaky biological speculations about the orgastic longings of protozoa, that human orgasm includes an attempt to become spherical, an attempt that man's possession of a backbone dooms to failure. How Reich arrived at such an idea, or why he should have wanted to maintain it, are entirely baffling problems, though as students of mysticism and theology know, Reich was not the first person to voice the existence of a wish to be spherical. According to an early Christian heresy, at the resurrection we will arise from the dead in the form of perfect spheres.

If one is capable of surmounting these various obstacles to taking Reich seriously, his account of vegetotherapy is not without interest and the technique is not so foolish as its theoretical trimmings. Starting from the two basic assumptions that 1) the aim of therapy is the release and restoration of the orgasm reflex, and 2) "every muscular rigidity contains the history and the meaning of its origin,"[3] Reich proceeded by picking on some stereotyped facial expression of the patient's and interfering with it, by, for instance, continually drawing the patient's attention to it, making him exaggerate it or adopt by an act of will the reverse expression. This apparently had two effects. The stereotyped expression

[2] *The Function of the Orgasm*, pp. 275–76.
[3] *Ibid.*, p. 267.

gradually became comprehensible as a compromise between two opposed forces: the wish to express an emotion, usually of anger or sorrow, and the wish to prevent
its expression. Interpretation of this conflict eventually
led to expression of the previously repressed emotion
and later to the patient remembering the childhood
traumatic experience which had engendered the emotion
and at the same time had necessitated its repression.
Second, tensions and rigidities in the patient's chest and
abdomen gradually became visible and palpable. (It is
not explicitly stated to what extent his patients were
undressed at this stage in the proceedings, but Reich
writes throughout as though their whole bodies were
visible to him and he several times reports himself as
palpating muscles and viscera.) These chest, abdom-
inal, and, later, pelvic tensions were then dealt with as
the earlier facial ones had been—and with similar releases of anger or tears. Then at some point in the proceedings the patient began to report pleasurable and
often unequivocally sexual sensations. These were the
first signs of the emergent orgasm reflex breaking out of
the character armor. In the one case which Reich de-
scribes in detail, the last phase of treatment consisted
in the patient's describing in minute detail his behavior
during the sexual act, including his discovery that his
pelvis could move by itself.

Characteristically, Reich remains silent both about
the patient's physical and psychological responses to
being looked at and touched by his therapist, and about
the therapist's responses to the increasing relaxation,
trustfulness, and overt sexual behavior of his patients.
He writes, as twenty-five years later Masters and John-

son have done, as though it were possible for a therapist to remain objective, unmoved, and yet human when confronted with the overt sexual reactions of his patients. As a result it is impossible to decide whether the effectiveness of such direct onslaughts on sexual inhibition depends on the therapist's correct under-standing of the psychological and physiological principles involved or on some charismatic factor in his personality that enables him to bless the patient sexually by a secular, pseudo-medical form of the religious ceremony of laying on of hands (confirmation).

Incidentally, Reich, unlike Masters and Johnson, does not appear to have found it necessary to supply "surro-gate partners" for patients without partners. (In their recent *Human Sexual Inadequacy* Masters and Johnson report doing so occasionally for unattached males who apply for treatment at the Reproductive Biology Re-search Foundation at St. Louis.)

In view of Reich's later development, his account of vegetotherapy contains one detail of great significance. This is that, concurrently with the dissolution of their character and muscular armors and the emergence of their true orgastic capacity, his patients regularly re-called, with deep emotion, a time in their childhood when they had felt at one with their surroundings, and recounted how this feeling of being alive and in har-mony both with themselves and with nature had been disrupted by their training.

In this passage, which is unfortunately too long to quote, Reich is, I think, doing something more than describe the loss of the neurotic sense of aliena-tion that occurs at the end of all successful psychotherapies, though I suspect that some of his patients would have been prepared to leave it at that. He is also proclaiming his own conviction that he had at last discovered, by what in his own view was a pure natural-scientific route, the rational basis of his earlier intimations of the oneness of self and nature and the reconciliability of Freud's mechanistic view of man and Bergson's vitalism.

It would, I think, have been better for Reich's reputation if he had stopped here and had contented himself with asserting that successful psychotherapy leads patients to a view of their relationship to nature which resembles the religious conception of pantheism. However, intransigent as ever, Reich felt obliged to search for some physical process by which this sense of the harmony between self and nature was mediated. As a young man, in the early 1920s, Reich had maintained that "there was no denying the principle of a creative power governing life; only it was not satisfactory as long as it was not tangible, as long as it could not be described or practically handled." In the late 1930s and early 1940s, following a number of very peculiar and unconvincing experiments conducted during the course of practicing vegetotherapy, Reich succeeded in persuading himself that he had indeed discovered something tangible which is present in both man and nature, which pervades the cosmos, and which is the active force responsible for man's longing for orgastic and mystical union with the Other. This something tangible Reich called "orgone energy," "bio-energy," or "primordial cosmic energy"; it was, he claimed, not only universally present but also universally demonstrable;

it could be seen under a microscope and its activities recorded with thermometers, electroscopes, and Geiger-Müller counters. It is, however, impossible to take this "discovery" of Reich's seriously, since he also maintained that "orgone energy" is a different sort of substance or phenomenon from those that microscopes, thermometers, electroscopes, and Geiger-Müller counters are constructed to observe and measure. In other words, he maintained that he had discovered a form of energy different in quality from the kind of energy with which the natural sciences concern themselves, but justified his "discovery" by an appeal to natural-scientific techniques. It is not surprising, therefore, that no scientist of any standing or merit has ever taken the slightest notice of Reich's researches; or that several of his friends, notably A. S. Neill and Nic Waal, went out of their way to assert their incompetence to pass judgment on his later work; or that his enemies dismissed his orgone theory as a paranoid delusional system and used it as evidence that he had been crazy all along.

There is, however, a more interesting and also more charitable way of approaching the system of ideas developed by Reich in his later years. This is to regard it not, as Reich himself claimed, as a scientific theory based on experimental researches, but as a philosophy of life, a *Weltanschauung*, perhaps even a cosmology or theology, which Reich arrived at by some unrecorded inner, private process of development. As I mentioned in my first chapter, in one respect Reich did not live up to his claim to have stepped "beyond the intellectual framework of present-day human character structure"; he never questioned the idea that rationalism and the natural sciences are the only avenue to the truth. As a result he formulated his system of ideas as though he had arrived at them by scientific techniques of observation and inference, a piece of self-deception that led him to exaggerate the originality of his ideas and to ignore their similarity to ideas that recurrently through history have been expressed by poets and mystics—and into making a number of very bizarre statements that, particularly when quoted out of context, do indeed often sound crazy.

In view of my conviction that the system of ideas that Reich himself styled the science of orgonomy really belongs to theology and mysticism and not to science, I shall attempt in the next chapter to describe them in a way that will draw attention to their resemblances to ideas previously voiced by poets and mystics, who themselves made no claim to have reached them by other than introspective means. I shall do so without dwelling too much on the absurdity of the pseudo-scientific language in which he expressed them. The reader is, however, warned that Reich's writings on orgonomy resemble other religious writings in raising problems of exegesis and hermeneutics, which make it possible for different readers to read different meanings into his writings. I gather that Reich's present-day followers do not agree among themselves on the correct interpretations to be put on his theories, or on which of his writings carry his central message.

vi

According to Reich, our civilization produces two types of human beings, mechanists and mystics. Mechanists are interested in material things and the natural sciences but have no spontaneous sense of life, while mystics, on the other hand, retain a sense of life but explain it supernaturally by reference to a "soul," which they conceive to have only an accidental, temporary, and regrettable connection with the body.

The division of mankind into mechanists and mystics is the result of an unexplained "original sin"—of which more later—that led mankind to develop a defensive armor against its own life forces. Mechanists are people who have turned completely against themselves, who have totally imprisoned their life forces within a defensive character armor, and who have as a result no awareness of their own true nature. Mystics, on the other hand, are people who have retained glimmering intimations of their own life force but who deny its origin in their own bodies and locate it in a hypothetical soul.

Since both mechanists and mystics have turned against the life of the body, science and religion have failed to recognize the significance of orgasm, that bodily experience in which physical pleasure and the sense of spiritual union with the infinite are at one with one another.

Furthermore, since orgasm unites the bodily and the spiritual, understanding of its essential nature makes it possible to break down the dichotomy between the mechanical and the mystical, the natural-scientific and the religious-poetic visions of reality, and to arrive at a *Weltanschauung* that embraces both. However, anyone who succeeds, as Reich claims he did, in achieving such understanding, finds that he is in the embarrassing position of having "stepped beyond the intellectual framework of present-day human character structure and, with that, the civilization of the last 5,000 years." He also incurs the hostility of both mechanists and mystics and becomes a threat to the established order. Indeed the two people who in Reich's opinion had anticipated his discoveries, Jesus Christ and Giordano Bruno, were both martyred. Since Bruno's life and ideas are not familiar to everyone, I should perhaps mention that he was burned at the stake in Rome for his adherence to pantheism. "His enthusiasm for nature, however, led him to hold an extreme form of pantheistic immanentism. God was the efficient and final cause of everything, the beginning, middle, and end, the eternal and infinite."[1]

The new form of thinking, feeling, and experiencing that arises when the significance of orgasm is fully understood was named by Reich "functional," this term being chosen by him to differentiate his position from that of the mystics. It indicates that organisms function the way they do simply because it is their nature to do so and not, as the mystics maintain, at the behest of some higher purpose or power. In particular, it is the nature of man—and indeed, as Reich eventually came to believe, of all living organisms and even parts of organisms—to strive for recurrent orgasm. A rose is a rose is a rose, and an orgasm is an orgasm is an orgasm.

It was not, however, Reich's belief that the orgasms with which most members of our society are familiar were examples of the successful fusion of the mechanical and mystical. On the contrary, he held that defensive armoring against sexuality and life forces was so widespread that the majority of human beings never experience orgasm in his sense of the word. "I say on the basis of ample clinical experience that only in a few cases in our civilization is the sexual act based on love. The intervening rage, hatred, sadistic emotions and contempt are part and parcel of the love life of modern man."

Reich's descriptions of orgasm and his interpretations and analyses of its function contain two metaphysical assumptions, which at times are explicit: that

[1] *The Oxford Dictionary of the Christian Church*, ed. F. L. Cross (London and New York: Oxford University Press, 1957).

the subjective and the objective are identical; and that the whole is contained in the part.[2]

If, to use an example used by Reich himself, we see spots in front of our eyes or have flickering sensations when we stare at the sky, these phenomena are not visual illusions but correspond to actual processes occurring in nature, and Reich devoted considerable energy and ingenuity to demonstrating that visual phenomena of this kind are really evidence of man's capacity to perceive, by reason of his vegetative harmony with nature, the bio-energy present in the sky and in nature generally—and that therefore bio-energy is ubiquitous, both immanently within the perceiving organism and externally. "Every perception is based on the consonance of a function in the outer world; that is, it is based on vegetative harmony."[3] So far as I understand this idea, it seems to me to be a pseudo-scientific formulation of the theological idea of the ubiquity of the Body of Christ; a belief that Luther held but that Kepler, who was otherwise a devout Lutheran, got into trouble for refusing to affirm.[4]

By a similar process of reasoning, Reich persuaded himself that all the subjective impressions of yearning and excitement experienced during orgasm correspond to real "bio-energetic" processes occurring not only in the subject's own body but also in nature at large. As a

[2] See *International Journal for Sex-Economy and Orgone-Research*, Vol. I (1942), and *Ether, God and Devil* (Rangely, Me.: Orgone Institute Press, 1951).
[3] *International Journal for Sex-Economy and Orgone-Research*, Vol. I (1942).
[4] See Arthur Koestler, *The Sleepwalkers* (New York: Macmillan, 1959).

result of this "functional identity" between the microcosm and the macrocosm, between the Self and the Other, even the verbal imagery used to describe the subjective sensations occurring before, during, and after orgasm can be used as valid evidence for elucidating what actually does happen during it, both inside the organism experiencing the orgasm and throughout the cosmos.

This functional mode of thinking, which, it must be emphasized, is only available to those who have succeeded in uniting the mystical and the mechanical, is, or so it seems to me, a pseudo-scientific version of Blake's statement that the innocent (i.e., the unarmored) can "see a world in a grain of sand and a heaven in a wild flower." According to Reich "a thundercloud in itself has nothing to do with an ameba. Still it is possible through the observation of definite functions in the ameba to draw conclusions which are also valid for the thundercloud, for instance, the attraction which is exercised by highly charged thunderclouds on smaller clouds just as it is exercised by an ameba on small bions."[5] (Bions are small packets or vesicles of bioenergy that Reich succeeded in seeing through a microscope.)

Since orgasm exemplifies and indeed in some sense contains within itself all living activity, analysis of its nature and course leads to complete understanding of the nature of life. The orgastic experience consists not only of tension followed by relaxation but also of a subjective sense of excitation followed by a feeling that

[5] *Ether, God and Devil.*

something has been discharged. This something cannot be semen, since the feelings of tension, excitation, and discharge are not confined to the genital organs and occur in women as well as in men. It must therefore be something else; at first Reich thought it was electricity, but later he decided that it was a previously unknown form of energy, "orgone energy" or "bio-energy," which he conceived concretely and claimed actually to have observed. Unlike Freud's libido, from which historically it derives, Reich's orgone energy is putatively an observable, "tangible" biological phenomenon (not an explanatory psychological concept), and according to Reichians it is "demonstrable visually, thermically, electroscopically and by means of Geiger-Müller counters."[6] It can also be stored in accumulators (orgone boxes). Almost all Reich's later researches consisted of attempts, in his view consistently successful, to demonstrate the real and universal presence of bio-energy and to demonstrate its efficacy in the treatment of not only neuroses but also psychosomatic disease and cancer. He also performed experiments that demonstrated to his own satisfaction that it could be used to control the weather.

Incidentally, orgone boxes—or to give them their official name "orgone-energy accumulators"—were constructed of alternating layers of steel wool and rock or glass wool, with celotex soft-board on the outside. Apparently they were the shape of a telephone box or coffin, and I am told that one did indeed feel a bit strange after being encased in one, probably on account of their poor ventilation.

[6] *Selected Writings*, p. 11.

Following the lead given him by quantum physics—and by Freud's idea that psychic energy exists in mobile and bound forms—Reich asserted that bio-energy exists in two forms: a mobile form consisting of mass-free pulsating vesicles (orgones); and a frozen or structured form, which has mass and is alive (bions). Mobile orgone energy is ubiquitous and identical with Primordial Cosmic Energy; structured orgone energy arises as a condensation or precipitation of mobile orgone energy first into transitional energy vesicles (bions) and later into living organisms (orgonomes). It would seem that Reich claimed both to have observed and induced experimentally the transformation of orgones into organisms, i.e., to have created life in the laboratory. One of the primary characteristics of orgones is pulsation; hence it is also the nature of orgonomes to pulsate. In doing so they generate further orgone energy, the accumulations of which are responsible for the recurrent need of all organisms for orgastic discharge.

Since an essential part of the subjective experience of orgasm is "longing to reach out beyond the narrow sack of one's own organism" and to merge with the "beyond of ourselves" (and not incidentally just with one's sexual partner), the orgone energy discharged during orgasm is "functionally identical" with love. The space-occupying but weightless vesicles discovered by Reich are quanta of the love proclaimed by the mystics and denied by the mechanists. Love, then, is no longer an idea or an ideal but something tangible, demonstrable "visually, thermically, electroscopically and by means of Geiger-Müller counters," and storable in orgone-energy accumulators. And since orgone energy is ubiquitous and resides both inside and outside ourselves, love too is everywhere, had we but Reich's faith to see it. Love is literally what makes the world go round.

> The moving primal orgone ocean appears as the primordial mover of the heavenly bodies. . . .
> The same energy which governs the movements of animals and the growth of all living substance also actually moves the heavenly bodies. . . .
> The physical Life Energy had been discovered in consequential pursuit of the functions of what is called "LOVE" in the whole animal kingdom.[7]

Incidentally, both cynics and romantics will be pleased to discover that love is blue.[8]

As a result of his discovery of the functional identity of orgone energy and love, Reich felt entitled to proclaim the unity of all antitheses!

> All boundaries between science and religion, science and art, objective and subjective, quantity and quality, physics and psychology, astronomy and religion, God and Ether, are irrevocably breaking down, being replaced by a conception of the basic unity.[9]

If the universe consisted solely of love (orgone energy), it would be a happy, joyous place, but as Reich well knew, it isn't. He had therefore to locate another form of energy, functionally identical with evil. This he found in nuclear radiation, which he conceived to be an entirely destructive, life-denying force. Fortunately, however, he succeeded in persuading himself that it

---

[7] *Ether, God and Devil*, and *The Oranur Experiment* (Rangely, Me.: Orgone Institute Press, 1951).
[8] See *Cosmic Superimposition* (Rangely, Me.: Orgone Institute Press, 1951).
[9] *The Oranur Experiment*.

could be neutralized by orgone energy and that therefore the forces of love are, in the long run at least, more
powerful than those of evil.

According to Robinson's essay on Reich[10] this conception of the universe as a battleground between life-
giving orgone energy and destructive nuclear radiation
is a modern, would-be scientific version of Manicheism
but, as I understand Reich, his position remained
basically within the Judeo-Christian tradition since he
also, or perhaps alternatively, postulated a destructive
form of orgone energy (DOR), which becomes "sequestered" from creative orgone energy and turns
against it. This sequestered destructive energy is the
force that character armor uses in its struggles to re-
press the organism's creative, orgastic strivings.[11] This
concept of DOR, which Reich must have derived from
Freud's idea that repression is maintained by "healthy"
aggressive energy being turned back against the self
(i.e., the superego using id-energies to combat the id),
seems to me to be "functionally identical" with the
theological idea that the Devil is an angel cast out of
heaven.

Curiously enough, DOR also manifests itself in clouds,
or rather accumulations of something invisible but
blighting that can overhang landscapes, especially
deserts and swamps, even when the sun is shining:

A "stillness" and "bleakness" spread over the landscape . . . expressed in a real cessation of life expressions in the atmosphere. The birds stop singing; the

10 In Paul A. Robinson, *The Freudian Left* (New York:
Harper & Row, 1969).
11 See *Orgone Energy Bulletin*, Vol. 4, No. 4 (October 1952).

frogs stop croaking. There is no sound of life any-
where. The birds fly low or hide in the trees. Animals
crawl over the ground with greatly reduced motility.
The leaves of the trees and the needles of the ever-
greens look very "sad"; they droop, lose turgor and
erectility. Every bit of sparkle or luster disappears
from the lakes and the air. It is not something that
"came into the landscape." It is, rather, the sparkle
of life that went out of the landscape.[12]

This is one of several passages in Reich which con-
vince me that, deeply repressed behind *his* scientific
character armor, was a nature poet struggling to escape.
"The sedge has withered from the lake/ And no birds
sing" wrote Keats; perhaps DOR and "La Belle Dame
Sans Merci" are not as unrelated as they seem.

Reich's discovery of the objective reality of love led
him inevitably but reluctantly to God.

He did not change his natural-scientific position; he
did not now believe that a personified or absolute
"spirit" governed the world. On the contrary: More
than ever his conviction was confirmed that there
exists and acts a *physical* power in the universe at the
roots of all being; a power or whatever you may call
it, which finally has become accessible to being
handled, directed, measured, put to useful purposes
by man-made tools. . . . "GOD," at this point, appeared
to be the perfectly logical result of man's awareness
of the existence of an objective, functional logic in
the universe.[13]

Although Reich has here reversed the relationship
traditionally assumed to exist between God and man—

[12] *Ibid.*
[13] *Cosmic Superimposition.* Despite the use of the third-
person singular, this passage is written by Reich himself.

man, it appears, created God, and Reich asserts that it is he who can handle and use God, not that man is a tool in God's hands—this passage has a curiously familiar ring about it. It has similarities with both the ideas of the "new" theologians of the Honest-to-God variety who define God as "the ground of our being" and with the form of pantheism which Wordsworth expressed openly in his "Lines Composed a Few Miles above Tintern Abbey" and which he carefully eliminated from *The Prelude*. (See Section 10 of Ernest de Selincourt's Introduction to the "uncensored" 1805 version.)

> And I have felt
> A presence that disturbs me with the joy
> Of elevated thoughts; a sense sublime
> Of something far more deeply interfused,
> Whose dwelling is the light of setting suns,
> And the round ocean and the living air,
> And the blue sky, and in the mind of man:
> A motion and a spirit, that impels
> All thinking things, all objects of all thought,
> And rolls through all things.

Reich's account, already quoted in the previous chapter, of how his patients "as small children [had] felt one with nature, with everything around them, how they felt 'alive,' and how all this was subsequently broken to pieces" is also paralleled by the opening verse of Wordsworth's "Intimations of Immortality" from *Recollections of Early Childhood.*

> There was a time when meadow, grove, and stream,
> The earth, and every common sight,
> To me did seem

Apparelled in celestial light,
The glory and the freshness of a dream.
It is not now as it hath been of yore;—
Turn wherese'er I may,
By night or day,
The things which I have seen I now can see no more.

Psychologically speaking, the parallels that can be drawn between Reich's "science" of orgonomy and Wordsworth's natural religion are, I suspect, not accidental. Both lost both their parents while they were still children, and it is tempting to interpret both Reich's attempt to prove scientifically that man is at one with the cosmos and Wordsworth's ecstatic experiences of a sense of complete oneness with Nature as attempts to overcome the resulting sense of alienation and desolation. The differences between the two men and the two systems of thought, which are indeed so striking as to make any comparison seem at first sight absurd, could be attributed to the fact that Wordsworth lost his parents before puberty, whereas Reich lost his at an age when he must have already been capable of experiencing orgasm. Incidentally, there is a passage in Book II of *The Prelude* (lines 266–84) which suggests that Wordsworth was fully conscious of the connection between his feelings for nature and his love for his mother, whereas there is nothing in Reich's writings to suggest that he ever linked his idealization of orgasm and of matriarchy with the tragedies of his own childhood.

Despite Reich's claim to have discovered a mode of thinking that resolves all antitheses and to have demonstrated experimentally the material basis of phenomena traditionally conceived in religious, mystical, or psychological terms, it must not be thought that he claimed to have solved all the riddles of the universe. On the contrary, there remained two which continued to puzzle and baffle him.

One was the differentiation of organisms into male and female. This defeated him completely, remaining a "riddle from the viewpoint of orgone physics."[14] His theories would indeed fit a unisex or homosexual universe as well (or as badly) as they do a heterosexual one, and it is remarkable that all his accounts of orgasm are modeled on the male's experience. He is also consistently "phallocentric," to use Ernest Jones's word for Freud's attitude toward female sexuality, in that he always emphasizes the outgoing, thrusting, penetrative aspects of sexual desire and never enclosing, receptive longings. On the other hand, his insistence that women have sexual needs and an innate longing for orgasm as strong as the male's, coupled with his contempt for the masculine concept of sexual prowess and his emphasis on the importance of "phallic tenderness," place him among the pioneers of women's sexual liberation. I must confess, however, that personally I think that there is something chilling about the way in which he explains sexual desire solely by reference to the subject's mounting internal tension without regard to the desirability—or desires—of the object—and about his emphasis on cosmic longing for union with the "beyond" and his failure to say much about longing for the person of the loved one.

14 *Ether, God and Devil.*

In her biography of her husband, Ilse Ollendorf Reich states that in practice Reich subscribed to the Victorian "double standard" of sexual morality. He had affairs in her absence but insisted on her being faithful to him. She also says that he was pathologically jealous—"I almost had to take an oath of fidelity before he would be satisfied." In view of the well-known connections between jealousy, paranoia, and unconscious homosexuality, it is also relevant that she reports that he never knowingly accepted a homosexual for treatment—"*Ich will mit solchen Schweinereien nichts zu tun haben.*"

The second problem to which Reich found no satisfying answer was the origin of man's tendency to turn against himself and to imprison himself in defensive armor. His failure to do so was undoubtedly a source of considerable intellectual embarrassment, since he realized clearly that his whole position depended on the assumption that man's "original sin" of self-rejection was unnecessary and reversible:

> Still the question of how the armoring of the human animal as the only animal species [to do so] came about remains with us, unsolved, overshadowing every theoretical and practical step in education, medicine, sociology, natural science, etc. No attempt is made here to solve this problem. It is too involved. The concrete facts which possibly could provide an answer are buried in a much too distant past.[15]

Nonetheless he does offer a solution, albeit with surprising and unusual tentativeness. It is that armoring is a side-effect of the development of reflective self-awareness. By becoming conscious and, furthermore,

[15] *Cosmic Superimposition.*

conscious of his capacity to be conscious, man began to treat himself as an object and to regard his urge to fuse with the beyond as a threat to his capacity to be conscious. "In thinking about his own being and functioning, man turned involuntarily against himself; not in a destructive fashion, but in a manner which may well have been the point of origin of his armoring."[16] As Reich himself realized, this explanation of the origin of character armor is basically a secular restatement of the religious idea that man's "original sin" was eating of the tree of knowledge.

Although this explanation is, I suspect, correct so far as it goes, it comes as something of an anticlimax. It amounts to little more than saying that self-awareness contains within itself the risk of becoming alienated both from others and from the instinctual self, or that surrendering oneself to one's passions and to the desire to fuse with the Other can be experienced as a threat to one's sense of identity. It seems sad that Reich should have spent such a tormented, persecuted, and futile life finding out something so obvious.

It is also a conclusion that makes nonsense of his belligerence toward both the mechanists and mystics, since on his own showing they are not villains, but victims of an inescapable hazard of the human condition. A new note of tolerance that can be detected in his later writings was presumably the result of his having realized this.

[16] *Ibid.*

Summing Up

vii

Since Reich is regarded in some circles as a
prophet and one of the great liberators of mankind, it remains for me to justify having, at the
end of the last chapter, described his life as
"tormented, persecuted, and futile."

The evidence that Reich was a tormented personality is provided by Ilse Ollendorf Reich's
biography—a disenchanted but sympathetic and
loyal book which rings true throughout. His
adored mother committed suicide when he was
fourteen, his less loved father died when he was
seventeen, his only sibling, a younger brother,
died before he was thirty. From an early age he
lost all contact with his origins in Bucovina.
Although he became a psychoanalyst while still
a medical student, his own experiences of being
analyzed were unfortunate; indeed one of his

analysts decamped for America without giving him any warning, leaving him, it is said, in the middle of a depression. He was restless, overactive, jealous, suspicious, and possessive, smoked and drank excessively—but A. S. Neill paints a different picture, describing him as relaxed but subject to rages, and says, equally contradictorily, that he never drank to excess since drink never seemed to affect him one bit. He also suffered from two diseases, tuberculosis and eczema, which may (but on the other hand may not) have been psychosomatic. He had little sense of humor and took himself and his work dead seriously. According to Neill he found small talk unendurable—"*Gesellschafts* conversation just means hell to me"—and his conversation was always about his work. He also always kept a distance between himself and others. As Neill says, "Reich always put up a barrier. He addressed his fellow workers as Dr. X or Dr. Y and they addressed him as Dr. Reich. I think that Ola Raknes of Oslo and I were the only friends and co-workers who addressed him as simply Reich!"

It seems, indeed, always to have been Reich versus the Rest and, with the exception of Freud, there seems to have been no one from whom he felt he had ever got support or inspiration. Intellectually, he seems always to have gone it alone; his writings convey no sense of dialogue with other minds; his disciples followed his lead but there is no indication that any of them contributed to the development of his thought; and his reading seems to have been directed more toward finding support for his own ideas than toward learning from others. All this suggests, I think, that he was an intrinsically lonely man, driven and tormented from within. One can only surmise that he was himself engaged in a lifelong but unsuccessful struggle to escape from his own defensive armor.

He also seems to have been remarkably unself-aware. Ilse Ollendorf Reich reports that he was socially naïve, overimpressed by academic titles but incapable of assessing, for instance, their different significance in the European and American scenes. As a result he often overestimated the academic standing of those who came to him for training. And, especially in someone who started life as a psychoanalyst, his obliviousness of his dynamic effect on others seems remarkable. It never seems to have occurred to him that his therapeutic successes may sometimes have been more a function of his personality than of his theories.

The fact that Reich was persecuted is shown by his career. He was expelled from both the International Psychoanalytical Association and the Communist movement. After he left Germany for political reasons, professional opposition made it impossible for him to work in Denmark and Norway. In the United States the Food and Drug Administration placed an injunction on the distribution of orgone-energy accumulators, and later he was imprisoned for contempt of court.

Reich seems consistently to have interpreted this persecution as evidence of the correctness of his ideas. As Ilse Ollendorf Reich emphasizes, he identified himself with Christ, whom he regarded as the archetypal "genital character," in direct contact with cosmic orgone energy, and viewed his own life as one of martyrdom. He considered his *The Murder of Christ* to be his most important book.

Finally there are, I think, four reasons why Reich's life must be adjudged a failure and futile—this despite the fact that in his lifetime he made a stir wherever he went and that he continues to be regarded as a prophet of sexual revolution.

First, it is precisely those of his ideas by which he set most store that have to be dismissed as bizarre and absurd. His psychological ideas on defense and character armor have, after a fashion, been assimilated by psychoanalysis and have become part of the intellectual equipment of therapists who are often unaware of their indebtedness to him, but even during his "orthodox" psychoanalytical phase there were two features of his work and attitude that failed to have any impact on the psychoanalytical movement. These were his optimism and his therapeutic belligerence. Reich believed that the neuroses were unnecessary artifacts produced by bourgeois society and parental suppression of infantile sexual activities, but almost all analysts have followed Anna Freud in holding that "the hope of extirpating neuroses from human life is . . . illusory." Nor have many analysts followed Reich in being forceful and aggressive in their attacks on their patients' character armor. Reich blitzed his patients' defenses with a relentlessness that most analysts would find offensive. And those few analysts who in private will admit that on occasion they do so, are generally reluctant to recommend such a technique publicly. When I was a student at the Institute of Psycho-Analysis in London in the 1940s, my training analyst lent me a typescript translation of Reich's *Der Triebhafte Charakter* (1925) as soon as I started treating patients, but I have no recollection of Reich being mentioned at formal lectures. And no English translation of *Der Triebhafte Charakter* has ever been published.

In view of the probability that Reich's contribution to the development of psychoanalysis has been greater than is generally recognized or admitted, it is of interest to note that in *Reich Speaks of Freud*[1] Reich gives a list of establishment analysts who in his opinion understood his message but elected to remain silent.

On the other hand, Reich's would-be scientific ideas about orgones and orgone energy have rightly been rejected as fanciful. From a scientific point of view, there is something pathetic about Reich's accounts of his experiments and theories. The experiments seem to have been designed and carried out in a hopelessly amateurish and gimcrack manner with, in particular, no understanding of the need for adequate controls, while his theorizing is full of the most elementary mistakes in biology and physics. One is left with the impression that Reich lacked, even as a young man, any appreciation of scientific method, and that his need to find "tangible" things to correspond with ideas indicated some defect in his capacity for conceptual thinking.

Second, if one takes Reich's life and works not as a scientific career but as a spiritual progress or peculiar form of theological inquiry, his conclusions were hardly original enough to justify the torment and persecution he went through in order to reach them. The ideas that

[1] The transcript of a discussion between Reich and Kurt R. Eissler published by the Noonday Press (New York, 1968) without the consent of either Eissler or the Sigmund Freud Archives, Inc.

God is not the creator of the universe but is the universe and that the objective and subjective are identical crop up recurrently in the theological tradition of Western civilization. His failure to realize this provides an example of his inability to engage in dialogue with other minds. As a result, he pursued a solitary and at times heroic path, oblivious of the fact that others had explored it before him.

Third, the prophetic, evangelical, and often strident tone of Reich's writings has led to his being remembered as more of an extremist and revolutionary than he perhaps ever was—and certainly more than he was in his later years. His intransigent advocacy of Marxism in psychoanalytical circles and of psychoanalysis within the Communist movement inevitably got him into trouble with both and gave him a reputation for intellectual bloody-mindedness that in retrospect hardly seems justified. Nowadays we find nothing incongruous or outrageous in attempts to reconcile Marx and Freud —indeed in certain quarters it seems to have become a fashionable exercise—or in suggestions that there may be some intrinsic connection between the social structure of a society and the psychological structure of its component members, but in the 1920s and 1930s in Central Europe Marxism was politics, not sociology, and in the minds of the professional middle classes Communism was linked with Nazism, both being regarded as part of a general revolt of the masses which was threatening civilization.

Reich's unacceptability to both the Communists and the analysts must have been enhanced by his assertions that a "deep-reaching revolution of cultural living"[2] was already in progress, which was the result of neither the class dialectic of history nor the impact of psycho-analysis. This revolution, which is "without parades, uniforms, drum or cannon salutes" and has led to "thorough disintegration of moralistic, ascetic forms of living," Reich attributed to technological changes which were reducing the authoritarian role of fathers and loosening family ties by taking women out of the home into industry. This again is a thesis that today seems commonplace; variations of it can be found in Marcuse's accounts of "late industrial society" and in Alexander Mitscherlich's *Society Without the Father.*

The later Reich's repudiation of his early political and sexual revolutionary positions seems to have been absolute. He became virulently anti-Communist and a fervent admirer of President Eisenhower, with whom indeed he believed he had a special, though secret relationship, and he also came to believe that attempts to introduce sexual freedom rapidly would do far more harm than good.

Fourth, Reich's insistence on making orgasm the foundation stone of his theories makes them liable to distortion and vulgarization. Although he seems consistently throughout his life to have believed that the liberation of man depended on society's attitude toward its children and adolescents—the former should be granted the freedom to explore their own bodies and the latter the privacy to establish premarital relation-

2 *The Sexual Revolution*, p. xiv.

ships—his theories can be construed as a justification for adult promiscuity, which he abhorred. At the end of his life he realized this threat to his ideas and feared that his authority would be invoked to unleash "a free-for-all fucking epidemic." He eventually replaced the term "orgasm" by that of "genital embrace" and even went so far as to justify Saint Paul's strictures on the Flesh on the ground that "He had to build strong dams against the pornographic, filthy, sick mind of man in sexual matters, even at the price of killing the true Christ."[3]

[3] *The Murder of Christ* (New York: Noonday Press, 1953), p. 193.

SHORT BIBLIOGRAPHY

INDEX

SHORT BIBLIOGRAPHY

Reich was an enormously prolific writer, but much of his work has never been translated into English, and much of what has is either out of print or was published in journals which were burned by the United States government. However, Mary Boyd Higgins in her *Wilhelm Reich: Selected Writings* (New York: Farrar, Straus & Cudahy, 1960) gives what purports to be a complete list of his writings, while Paul Edwards in his article on Reich in *The Encyclopedia of Philosophy* (New York: Macmillan, 1967) gives an extensive though incomplete bibliography both of Reich's own writings and of the critical literature related to it.

To confine oneself to books that are in print and readily available, Reich's contributions to orthodox psychoanalysis can be deduced from the three original versions of papers written by him before his expulsion from the psychoanalytical movement, which are included in Robert Fliess's *The Psychoanalytic Reader* (London: Hogarth, 1950). Full and indeed repetitive accounts of his theory of sex economy and his attempts to reconcile psychoanalysis and Marxism can be found in his own *Character Analysis* (New York: Farrar, Straus & Young, 1949), *The Function of the Orgasm* (New York: Noonday Press, 1942), and *The Sexual Revolu-*

tion (4th rev. ed., New York: Farrar, Straus & Giroux, 1969); and in Paul Edwards's article. Extensive extracts from Reich's orgonomic "religious" writings are given in Mary Boyd Higgins's *Selected Writings*. Reich's *The Murder of Christ* and *Listen, Little Man!* are also readily obtainable but should be avoided by anyone who wishes to retain any respect for him.

Biographical data about Reich can be found in Ilse Ollendorf Reich, *Wilhelm Reich: A Personal Biography* (New York: St. Martins Press, 1969); Paul Ritter, ed., *Wilhelm Reich* (Nottingham: Ritter Press, 1958), which was published in a limited edition and is not easily available; and Higgins and Raphael, eds., *Reich Speaks of Freud* (New York: Noonday Press, 1968).

INDEX

Abortion, 6, 60

Abstinence, sexual, 24, 57

Adolescence, sources of neurosis in, 57–60

Adolescents, 101–102; sex suppressed in, 36, 61; sexual intercourse for, 59–60

Adulthood, sources of neurosis in, 60–62

Affluence, 64

Aggressiveness, 30

Alienation, 74, 93

Analyst, patient's relation to, 23, 68

Andréas-Salomé, Lou, 15

Anthropology, 47–48

Antitheses, 86, 90

Anxiety, 29, 35

Ardrey, Robert, 30

Austro-Hungarian Empire, 1, 2

Authority, submissiveness to, 43

Autonomic nervous system, 70–71

Bachofen, J. J., 49

Bateson, Gregory, 42

Beethoven, Ludwig van, 8

Bergson, Henri, 17, 75

Bio-energy, 16, 75, 82, 84. *See also* Libido

Bions, 11, 83, 85

Birth control, 6, 60, 64

Blake, William, 16, 83

Body contractions, involuntary, 26

Brother Animal: The Story of Freud and Tausk (Roazen), 5n

Brücke, Ernst, 13

Bruno, Giordano, 80–81

Cancer, 12, 33

Capitalism, 64

Causation and mental phenomena, 14

Celibacy, 38

Character: in authoritarian mold, 36; concept derived from Freud, 18; as defense, 22, 23, 24, 54; neurosis, 27; structure, 43–44, 76

Character analysis, 23

Character Analysis, 6, 7

Character and Anal Erotism (Freud), 23

Character armor, 24, 27, 28, 33, 88, 98; as defense, 40, 54, 55, 87; and inhibition of orgastic potency, 37; against life forces, 78, 79; and muscular tension, 40, 67–68, origin, 92–93; released, 73, 74; as result of patriarchal society, 35, 41–42

Childbirth, 60

Childhood: sources of neurosis in, 54–57. *See also* Infancy

Children, 63, 101

Civilization, 20n, 78

Civilization and Its Discontents (Freud), 19–20

"Civilized Sexual Morality and Modern Nervousness" (Freud), 20

Class structure and morality, 64

Coitus interruptus, 24

Communism, 7; and Nazism, 100; primitive, 50; Reich's commitment to, 45–46

Communist Party, 4, 7; Austrian, 5, 6; German, 5, 6, 44

Compassion, 40

Conscious, the, 15

Consciousness, 14

Contraceptives, 60, 64

Conversion, 29

Cosmic Superimposition, 88n

Cosmos, orgasmic functional identity with, 83

Countertransference, 24

Culture; character armor and, 40; Freud's theory of, 20; patriarchal, authoritarian, 46; Reich's attitude to, 40; sexual customs, 58

Danger of Equality, The (Gorer), 59

Da Vinci, Leonardo, 8

Death instinct concept, 31, 41, 43

Defense: character as, 18, 22, 54; and character armor, 39, 41, 54–55, 98; patient's, against analyst, 23

Demand feeding, 56

Depression, 55

De Selincourt, Ernest, 89

Despair, 55

Destructiveness, 31

Dialectical Materialism and Pyschoanalysis, 6

Dominance, 52

Double bind theory, 42

Dreams, 23

Du Bois-Reymond, Emil, 13–14

Duty, 36; and character armor, 40; marital, 47

Ego, 15, 20n; defenses, 22; function of, 18, 19

Ego and the Id, The (Freud), 15

Ego Psychology and the Problem of Adaptation (Hartmann), 21n

Eisenhower, President Dwight D., 101

Eissler, Kurt R., 99n

Energy: aggressive, 87; biological, 16; bound, 16; discharge of, 15, 18; erotic, 16; life, 11; mental, Freud's theory of, 14–15, 17; mobile, 16; psychic, 85; sexual, 25, 29. *See also* Bio-energy; Orgone energy; Primordial cosmic energy

Engels, Friedrich, 49

Eros and Civilization (Marcuse), 40

Evolution of society, 48

Facial expression, in therapy, 72–73

Family; authoritarian, 36, 37, 41, 42, 43; pressure from, 41; psychiatry for, 42; structure, 43–44

Fascism, 7, 43

Fathers, 63; authoritarian, 101; pathogenic power, 42;

Primal, 47; repressive, 37, 41

Fox, Robin, 51

Frazer, Sir James, 49

Free association, 23

Freud, Anna, 98

Freud, Sigmund, 10, 38, 47, 49, 54, 85, 87, 91; death instinct theory, 41; ego defense concept, 18, 22; Marxism and, 100; mechanistic view of man, 75; mental energy, theory of, 14–18; neurosis, theory of, 24–25, 29; pessimism of, 19; and psychoanalysis, 13, 31; relations with Reich, 3, 5, 6; sublimation, 20n

Freudian Left, The (Robinson), 45n, 87n

Friendship, 60

Function of the Orgasm, The, 6, 17, 21–22, 27, 34, 35, 53, 56n, 70

Genital character, 21–22, 28, 30

Genital embrace, 102

Genitals, 26, 29

German Association for Proletarian Sexual Politics, 6

German Psychoanalytic Society, 7

Ghost in the Machine, The (Koestler), 44

God, rediscovered, 78, 88–89, 100

Gorer, Geoffrey, 59*n*
Grief, 55
Guilt, 50

Hatred, 24, 30
Helmholtz School of Medicine, 13–14
Holons, 44
Homosexuality, 60, 92
Human Sexual Inadequacy (Masters and Johnson), 74

Id; 15, 18–19, 20*n*
Identity, sense of, 93
Infancy: relationship with mother in, 55–56; sexuality suppressed in, 36, 98; sexual phantasies in, 25, 29; trauma, 9. *See also* Childhood
Infantile neurotic behavior in later life, 57
Inhibitions, sexual, 25, 64, 74
Instincts, 19, 33; and evolution, 31; expression of, 19; renunciation of, 20
Institute of Psychoanalysis, 98
International Journal for Sex-Economy and Orgone Research, 82*n*
International Psychoanalytic Association, 4, 97
International Psychoanalytic Publishing House, 6
"Intimations of Immortality" (Wordsworth), 89–90

Jealousy, 63; Reich's, 92
Jesus Christ, 8, 80–81, 102; Body of, 82; as genital character, 97; Reich's identification with, 97
Johnson, Virginia, 28, 73–74
Jones, Ernest, 20, 31, 91

Kepler, Johannes, 82
Kinsey, Dr. Alfred, 28
Kinship, 49
Klein, Melanie, 55
Koestler, Arthur, 44, 82

Laing, R. D., 24*n*, 55
Lawrence, D. H., 27
Leninism, 46
Libido, 16, 17, 27; compared to orgone energy, 84; and sadism, 29–30; undischarged, converted to anxiety, 29. *See also* Bio-energy
Life and Works of Sigmund Freud (Jones), 20*n*
Life force(s), 17; defensive armor against, 79–80, 81
Lineage, 49, 51; matrilineal, 50
"Lines Composed a Few Miles Above Tintern Abbey" (Wordsworth), 89
Lorenz, Konrad, 30
Love, 24, 28, 30, 58–59, 63; and mental illness, 35; objective reality of, 88; orgone energy and, 85; sexual act based on, 81

Lowen, Alexander, 24*n*
Luther, Martin, 82

"Make Love Not War," as Reichian slogan, 30
Malinowsky, Bronislaw, 50–51
Manicheism in Reich, 87
Manics, 38
Marcuse, Herbert, 40, 101
Marriage: as legal institution, 63, 64; monogamous compulsive, 57; as source of neurosis, 61
Marx, Karl, 50, 64
Marxism, 5; and psychoanalysis, reconciled, 4, 42, 43; Reich's, 4, 5, 9, 100
Masochism, female, 26
Masses: oppression of, 42–43; revolt of, 100
Mass media, 64
Mass Psychology of Fascism, The, 6
Masters, Dr. William, 28, 73–74
Masturbation, 24 45, 54; as compulsive symptom, 56; suppressed in infants, 56
Matriarchy, 47, 51–52, 90. *See also* Society
May, Rollo, 24*n*
Melanesians, 58
Mental health, 37; and orgastic potency, 37, 38; preconditions, 39
Mental illness, organic, 39

Mind, Freud's concept, 18–19
Mitscherlich, Alexander, 101
Monogamy, 61–62
Morality, 47; compulsive, 21, 24; permissive no threat to property, 64
Morgan, L. H., 49
Mothers: early oral attachment to, 55; schizophrenogenic, 42; working, 63
Murder of Christ, The, 97, 102
Muscular armor, 67, 68, 71, 74. *See also* Character armor
Muscular spasms, chronic, 35
Muscular tension and character armor, 37, 40, 67, 71
Mysticism, 77
Mystics, 78–81

Nature, 28; orgasm related to, 82–83; patients' relationship with, 75
Nazism, 100
Neill, A. S., 68, 70, 76, 96
Neurosis, 21, 55, 59, 64, character armor and, 67–68; family as factor in, 42; Freud's theory, 24; as holistic structure, 44; and lack of orgastic potency, 27–29; Reich's theory, 25–26, 34, 43; prevention, 54; and psychoneurosis, 24–26; unnecessary, 98

Noble Savage, the, 21
Nuclear radiation, 86–87

Oedipus complex, 9, 25, 46, 50; origin, 47, 49
Orgasm, 24–25, 27–28, 34, 101; as attempt to become spherical, 72; and the cosmos, 82, 83; essentials of, 85; frustrated, 25, 29–30; and mental health, 33, 37, 60; needs of healthy individuals, 62; and orgone energy, 83–85; Reich's theory based on male experience, 91; released from character armor, 73; significance of, 80–81; women's need for, 91
Orgastic potency, 26; absent in neurotics, 27, 29; preconditions, 39; and psychic health, 35, 38–39
Orgone energy, 75–76, 84–85, 99; sequestered, 87
Orgone-energy accumulators (orgone boxes), 11–12, 84
Orgones, 85, 99
Orgonomes, 85
Orgonomy, 77, 78–93
Original sin, 78, 92

Pantheism, 80, 89
Parents, 55, 60; authoritarian behavior, 36; honesty in, 69
Patients, 23, 75, 98
Paul, Saint, 102
Perls, F. S., 24*n*

Personality and sexual relationships, 21
Pfister, Oscar, 15
Phallic tenderness, 91
Physiology and psychopathology, 26
Polygamy, natural, 61
Poole, Roger S., 48
Posture, 37
Poverty, 53
Power, 64; oppressive, of father, 37; psychology of, 30
Pregnancy, 60
Prelude, The (Wordsworth), 89
Premarital relationships, 101
Primordial cosmic energy, 75–76, 85
Privacy, lack of, 53
Project for a Scientific Psychology (Freud), 16
Proletariat, 64
Promiscuity, 102
Property, 63; permissive morality no threat to, 64
Psychoanalysis: anal erotism and, 5, 54; and Marxism, 4, 42, 100; orgastic frustration and, 30–33; Reich's contribution to, 4–5, 99; social implications, 5; and vegetotherapy, 67–77
Psychoanalytic Reader, The (Fliess), 4, 5*n*
Psychoneurosis, 24–25; and incapacity to love, 39; and neurosis, 25, 26
Psychoneurotics, 22

Psychopathology and physiology, 26

Psychosis, family factor in, 42

Psychosomatic disease and orgone energy, 84

Psychotherapy: Reich's influence on, 5, 24; successful, 75; therapeutic effect of, 23

Puberty, 54, 57–59

Raknes, Ola, 96

Recollections of Early Childhood (Wordsworth), 89–90

Reich, Ilse Ollendorf, 1, 2, 4*n*, 92, 94, 97

Reich, Wilhelm: American citizenship, 1; antiauthoritarian attitude, 56; anti-Communism, 101; Austrian army service, 3; in Berlin, 6, 97; biography, 1–12; and Communist Party, 6, 44; death, 11–12; in Denmark, 11, 97; double-standard advocate, 92; family, 1–2, 94; father, 1, 94; and Freud, 3, 5, 6, 17, 29, 54; God rediscovered, 78, 88–89; holistic thinking, 44–45; and International Psychoanalytic Association, 4, 6, 97; later work, 16, 84, 93; loneliness, 2, 96; Marxism, 4, 5, 9, 46, 100; as medical student, 3; mother, 2–3, 94; and nature, 2, 88; in Norway, 11, 97; optimism of, 19, 21, 34; originality, lack of, 99; personality defects, 8, 94, 95; phallocentricity, 91; practicality, 34, 53; promiscuity abhorred by, 102; psychoanalysis and psychotherapy, contributions to, 4–5, 24, 99; psychoanalysis and sexology, early papers on, 3; reconciliation of psychoanalysis and Marxism, 43; repetitiveness, 36–37; repudiation of early views, 101; Russian visit, 6; sanity questioned, 8, 12, 92; and scientific method, 9–10, 99; secular upbringing, 2; and Seminar for Psychoanalytic Therapy, 4; as therapist, 68–70, 97; trial and imprisonment, 11–12, 97; in United States, 11–12, 97; utopianism, 33–34; as vitalist, 17, 75

Reich Speaks of Freud (Higgins and Raphael), 45, 99

Religion, 43

Repression, 18, 46; genital, 47; sexual, 50; and social oppression, 59

Reproductive Biology Research Foundation, 74

Respiration, inhibition of, 72

Ritter, Paul, 68*n*

Roazen, Paul, 5
Robinson, Paul A., 44, 45*n*, 87

Sadism: and libido, 29–30; male, 26
Schizophrenics, 38, 42
Schmitt, Vera, 56
School, authoritarian, 43
Self-awareness, 14, 34, 92–93
Self-destruction, 31
Self-regulation: inherent tendency to, 55; of organism, 21
Sex: and the genital character, 21; normal, 26; prime importance of, 27. *See also* Orgasm
Sex economy, 33, 34–35, 37, 64, 67; reforms based on Reich's theory, 54
Sexual act: analysis of, 27–28; based on love, 81
Sexuality: defensive armor against, 81; female, 91; infant, repressed, 41, 56, 61; repressed, 31
Sexual perversion, 39, 47
Sexual relationships: and loss, 5, 55; permanent, 62–63, 64
Sexual revolution, 50, 98; already occurred, 63–64; upper-middle-class phenomenon, 65
Sexual Revolution, The, 34, 45*n*, 53, 56, 57–58, 59*n*, 60

Sexual stasis, 21, 25, 57
Sleepwalkers, The (Koestler), 82*n*
Socialist Society for Sex Consultation and Sexological Research, 6
Social theory, 44–45, 46–50
Society: attitude toward youth, 101–102; bourgeois, 46, 54–55; as cause of sex chaos, 35; and character structure, 43; matriarchal, 46; matrilineal, 49, 50; pressure from, 41; primitive, 46, 48, 49; structure, 43–44, 49
Society Without the Father (Mitscherlich), 101
Spencer, Herbert, 48
Stalinism, 46
Storr, Anthony, 30
Sublimation, 20*n*
Superego, 15, 19, 87
Symptom analysis, 23

Tausk, Viktor, 5
Territoriality, 30
Theology, 76
Therapist: honesty of, 69; personality, 74
Therapy, to release orgasm reflex, 72
Toilet-training, 54
Totem and Taboo (Freud), 47
Totemism (Lévi-Strauss), 48*n*
Transference, 24, 68

Trauma, 9, 25
Triebhafte Charakter, Der, 98–99
Trobriand islanders, 50–51

Unconscious, the, 15; Reich's theory of, 70
United States Food and Drug Administration, 12, 97
Unity: of all antitheses, 85; man's longing for, 36
Universe, Reich's concept of, 86–87

Vegetotherapy, 67–77
Vienna, 4, 11, 13

Vienna Psychoanalytical Society, 3
Vitalism, 17, 75

Waal, Nic, 68–70, 76
Wilheim Reich (Ritter), 68n
Wilhelm Reich Infant Trust Fund, 11
Winnicott, D. W., 55
Women: economic independence of, 65, 101; need for orgasm, 91; protected by marriage, 62; social pressure on, 61; sources of love, 52
Wordsworth, William, 89–90